INSIGHT COMPACT GUIDE

FINLAND

KU-021-013

Compact Guide: Finland is the ultimate quick-reference guide to the land of the Midnight Sun. It tells you everything you need to know about this fascinating country, from the Lake Region to Lapland, the Same people to the sauna, modern designs to musical museums, and forest-covered fells to fast-flowing rapids.

This is one of 130 Compact Guides, combining the interests and enthusiasms of two of the world's best-known information providers: Insight Guides, whose innovative titles have set the standard for visual travel guides since 1970, and Discovery Channel, the world's premier source of nonfiction television programming.

APA PUBLICATIONS
Part of the Langenscheidt Publishing Group

Star Attractions

An instant reference to some of Finland's most popular tourist attractions to help you on your way.

Helsinki, p20

Turku, p28

Rauma, p41

The Lake Region, p47

Jyväskylä, p47

Kuopio, p50

Karelia, p56

Kilpisjärvi, p62

Rovaniemi, p63

Lapland, p65

Åland Islands, p69

FINLAND

Introduction

Places

Culture

Leisure

Practical Information

Finland – Land of a Thousand Lakes

Finland is a land of all seasons. Its blue-and-white flag is said to represent the white snow of winter and the blue lakes of summer. In between the two is the dramatic spring when everything turns green in a week, and autumn, full of reds and browns as the leaves swirl over the city squares.

The country has been independent since 1917. Before that time it was governed for centuries by foreign powers – Sweden and then Russia – and the struggle simply to survive has characterised much of its war-torn history. Finland is certainly Scandinavia's least understood and most culturally remote country.

The Finnish language was discouraged by the Swedes until the 19th century, when the famous *Kalevala*, a collection of folk tales, was written by Elias Lönnrot in 1835 *(see page 77)*; it instantly formed the basis for a clearly recognisable Finnish national culture. This was also reflected in the National Romantic movement in the arts, which flourished from the second half of the 19th century onwards. In addition to this, the music of Jean Sibelius gave the country a truly unique voice of its own.

Dressed to dance

Most of Finland is flat, and covered with lakes and forests, but the country can be divided up into clearly recognisable regions. In the south there's Helsinki, with harmonious architecture and many museums; the enormous lake region to the north of the capital is a centre of both industry and tourism; Ostrobothnia, to the west, is popular for its sandy beaches and magnificent old buildings, and is the home of the minority Swedo-Finns, whereas Lapland in the far north is a hiker's dream, with crashing rivers, lonely fells, unique Same culture and also the famous Midnight Sun *(see page 12)*. It's this part of Finland above all else which most resembles the music of Sibelius – haunting and majestic.

Vernacular style in Keuruu

5

Åland coastline

Position and size

Finland is made up of 11 provinces and the autonomous Åland Islands. It lies on the same latitude as Iceland, and one quarter of the country is inside the Arctic Circle. Its northernmost point is at 70°5', the southernmost at 59°30' (on the same latitude as Oslo), the westerly point at 19°7' and the easternmost at 31°35' (on the same line of longitude as Ankara). It is bordered in the north by Norway, in the northwest by Sweden, in the west by the Gulf of Bothnia, in the south by the Gulf of Finland and in the east by Russia. The country covers a total surface area of 338,000sq km (130,550sq miles), and its coastline is some 4,600km (2,760 miles) long.

Fabled forest

Topography

Finland is covered by a mixture of forest and marshland, and contains around 188,000 lakes and thousands of islands, almost enough, it seems, for every Finnish family to have an island or lake of their own, with plenty of space for visitors, too. Inland lakes cover almost 10 percent of the country's entire area; the largest lake, Saimaa, in the southeast, occupies roughly 4,400sq km (1,700sq miles). None of Finland's lakes are very deep, however; most of them average around 100m (330ft).

The landscape is mostly flat in the south, then it gradually rises and in the extreme northwest, near the Norwegian border, there are several high peaks including Mount Haltia, Finland's highest mountain (1,328m/4,357ft). The longest of Finland's many rivers is the Kemijoki (512km/343 miles) on the western coast, which flows into the Gulf of Bothnia.

The bedrock beneath Finland consists of an enormous granite shield, dating from the Precambrian era some 4,600 million years ago. The Ice Age had a marked effect on the relief of the country. As the glacier retreated, it left several deposits behind in the form of eskers (ridges of sand and gravel); among the largest of these are the Salpausselkä ridges in the south. Areas that were released from the weight of the massive ice sheets are still rising gradually even today; the whole country is actually emerging from the sea, at a rate of around 9mm (half an inch) every year.

The glaciers left behind many clays and silts, and these provide Finland with much of its fertile soil. The marshy northern third of the country is covered with layers of peat; this kind of soil covers around 30 percent of the country's total surface area.

Climate

Warm summers and cold winters

Finland's proximity to the Arctic Circle gives it warm summers and cold winters. In the summertime the temperature can often climb as high as 30°C (86°F), even in the northernmost parts of Lapland. Summer in southern Finland features the highest average temperatures in Northern Europe, easily on a par with Holland or Belgium. Temperatures in winter can often fall below -30°C (-22°F); in February they generally fluctuate between -30°C (-22°F) and -15°C (5°F).

Surprisingly little rain falls in Finland, with 30 to 40 percent of the annual precipitation falling as snow. From November to April much of the country lies beneath a white blanket of snow; in Lapland winter starts as early as October, and does not end until May. The dry air makes the low temperatures bearable, however. Spring is late, but when it arrives the snow melts incredibly quickly, and autumn is very colourful – especially in Lapland, when the first frost covers the leaves and the forests are a sea of yellow, red and brown.

The best time for winter sports enthusiasts to go to Finland is between mid-March and the end of April. In summer, it's worth remembering that the Finns tend to go on holiday from early July to mid-August, and many of the rural areas can become quite crowded – so plan a visit on either side of those times if at all possible. North of Rovaniemi, the Midnight Sun can be seen for two months during midsummer; the rest of Finland has a night-long twilight from June to July.

Getting around in winter

The People

The 'Nordic' image of a person with blond hair and blue eyes is quite a rare sight in Finland; most of the population is dark-haired. This is because of the Finns' ancestry: the people who moved into the southwestern corner of today's Finland from Estonia via the Baltic are referred to as 'trans-Ural nomadic'. Three tribes settled in different areas; the Suomalaiset (the Finns' word for themselves) decided to remain in the southern coastal provinces, and quickly altered their nomadic lifestyle; the Häme people settled the lake region, and the Karelians settled the forest regions to the east.

Finns don't conform to the Nordic image

The name 'Finland' dates back to Roman historian Tacitus (AD55–120). In his work *Germania* he mentioned a primitive people from the north called the Fenni, which was probably a reference to the Same *(see below)*, who at that time were living on and around the 60th parallel. Over the centuries the Same were gradually pushed further north, and today they live in Finnish Lapland.

Whichever part of the country they happen to come from, Finns have a lot in common: they all share deeply ingrained down-to-earth rural values combined with the spiritual qualities relating to the sauna. Many of them come from the land of Karelia which was split right down the middle by the Finno-Russian frontier in 1940, and after World War II; fewer people live there now, but the Karelians' pride at being something quite separate from either Finns or Russians still remains.

The Same

The Same are often referred to as Lapps, though they never use the term themselves since it was coined by their conquerors. They were herding reindeer as long as 4,000 years ago, and lived by hunting and fishing in Southern Scandinavia for a further 2,000 years.

There are no words in the Same language for 'war' or 'violence'; though whether the Same have always had a peaceful existence is another matter. Gradually pushed further and further north over the centuries, they have now finally found their home where no-one else wants to live: in an area measuring around 100,000sq km (38,600sq miles), situated roughly 100km (60 miles) north of the Arctic Circle, and shared today by Norway, Sweden, Finland and Russia.

Interest in the Same arose when traders realised the value of the furs and minerals in the region around Lake Pakasaivo *(see Route 9, page 61)*. Since the nomadic Same did not officially own the land and had no recognised territory, the conquerors had no problem in collecting taxes and declaring the land their own. The church – which had converted the Same to Christianity – and the 'crown' still allowed the Same to carry on hunting and fishing, and herding reindeer.

After Finland became an autonomous Russian grand duchy in 1809, the Same lost many of their rights. Today, the Finnish state continues to claim the land traditionally owned by the Same without the legal right to ownership. It was only after World War I that some initial efforts were made to respect Same rights. Paradoxically, several Same now consider that a life subsidised by the state is a lot more comfortable than herding reindeer as their forefathers did; this represents yet another threat to Same independence.

The Same way of life went through its biggest upheavals from the 19th century onwards: tents were replaced by solid housing, machines and motorised sledges were introduced, and the reindeer meat industry rapidly grew. A sub-group numbering only 600 people known as the Skolt Same lived from the mid-19th century until World War II in the Petsamo region of the Kola Peninsula. When the region was given up by Finland to the Soviet Union, the Skolt Same settled to the northwest of Lake Inari in the village of Sevettijärvi *(see Route 11, page 67)*, where each family owns its own lake.

Despite their conversion to Christianity by monks of the Russian Orthodox faith, the Skolt-Same have preserved their 'pagan' rites – many of which correspond remarkably with Christian festivals – far more successfully than other Same tribes. They are also considered to be closer to nature, wear their own form of traditional dress and stick stubbornly to their ancient traditions of transhumance, hunting and reindeer herding.

Preservation of cultural identity is very important to Finland's Same minority. Schools and the media are feeling the effects of this renewed interest in Same traditions; ancient Jolku songs telling of birth and death are being revived. The legends of the Inari-Same are passionate and heroic, but those of the Skolt-Same, famed for their prowess as singers and actors, are even more lyrical.

8

Preserving the Same culture

Church interior, Saltvik

Language

Finnish is one of the strangest and most difficult languages in the world. It belongs to the 'Finno-Ugric' family of languages, which is thought to have originated near the Ural Mountains. The official languages in Finland are Finnish, spoken by the majority people, and Swedish, though the latter is becoming increasingly less important. Estonian is closely related to Finnish; Hungarian is a more distant linguistic relative. Around 2,000 Same still speak their own language. The Northern Same language, also related to the Finno-Ugric family, is the most common form, followed by Inara Same and Skolt Same. The Same language is also being used increasingly in the media and in schools.

Religion and demography

Around 60 percent of Finland's total population of just over 5 million people live in cities and towns, and 40 percent in rural areas. Most Finns (nearly 86 percent) are Lutheran Protestants; there is also a small Russian Orthodox minority (1 percent). The rest belong to other churches, or are not affiliated.

International relations

Throughout its history Finland has found itself positioned between the Western and Eastern political and cultural spheres of influence. Geopolitics has, however, limited Finland's freedom of movement as a state. The policy of neutrality pursued during the Cold War did not allow Finland to join any Western European organisation that could be construed to promote the political values and objectives of the Western allies. One such organisation was the Council of Europe (which Finland joined in 1989), and another the European Economic Community (EEC).

When the country became a member of the European Union (EU) in 1995, it had at last taken its rightful place in the community of Western European nations. At the same time, Finland continues to enjoy a good political relationship with Russia and is keen to benefit from its position as a gateway between Russsia, the EU and other parts of the West in the provision of a range of services, including transportation and logistics. Trade between Finland and Russia, which collapsed with the dissolution of the Soviet Union, has been revitalised and acquired new forms as Russia's economic reform process advances.

Government

Until recently, Finland's parliamentary democracy was based on a consensus being reached between a strong president and the workers and unions. The parliament, re-elected every four years, and the prime minister – appointed by the president – were not considered to be the real centre of power.

The leading position of the president in the field of foreign policy, which is part of the Finnish political system, was also exaggerated during the Cold War. Membership of the EU has increased the responsibilty of the prime minister and his government for they now manage Union matters in addition to home affairs.

Economy

Until World War II Finland's economy was predominantly agricultural, though forestry and mining were important. Stalin seized 25 percent of Finland's pulp industries in 1940 and a similar share of other industries based in Karelia. It was only when the Treaty of Friendship and Co-operation was signed with Russia in 1948 that the way was opened for industrial production; this mainly involved mechanical engineering equipment which helped to pay off war reparations and rebuild the country's infrastructure.

Reaping the harvest
Bound for the sawmill

Finland did much brisk trade during this so-called 'Russian era', and even when all the reparations had been met, Finnish products were still in great demand. The country then began to exchange its industrial products for Soviet crude oil, and its trade with its neighbours in the East increased rapidly.

This industrial development has now given way to a services and information-oriented economy, largely based on free enterprise, though the government does retain a monopoly in a number of sectors including the airlines, the railways and the oil and gas industries.

Although Finland developed into a modern industrial state far later than other countries in Northern and Central Europe, the results so far have been impressive. Metalworking and mechanical engineering are the main industries; the principal manufactured products include mobile phones, sawmill machinery, icebreakers, luxury cruise liners, generators and cables. The wood and paper industry has also concentrated on high-quality products such as furniture, packaging material and special paper. The country's leading exports include furs, of which it is the largest exporter in the world, as well as textiles, glass and porcelain.

11

As recently as 1990, the Finnish state was still spending up to 20 percent of the country's GDP on maintaining the standard of living and adequate social services. The economic crisis that hit the country immediately after the dissolution of the Soviet Union led to a sharp reduction in public spending, but recently Finland has seen an upswing and today the country ranks among the most successful in Europe.

Flora and fauna

No other country in the world has more marshland than Finland; it is as distinctive a feature of the country as the famous Finnish lakes. The moors – often severely mosquito-ridden – yield harvests of cloudberries *(lakka)*, which are used to make a special liqueur.

A large part of the country is covered with coniferous forest, but in the south there are also several species of deciduous tree including birch, maple and elm. Most of the conifers in Finland are either pine or spruce. Plant life is not all that varied, but there are several kinds of edible fungi in the forests and many types of berry.

Finland's wildlife is alive and well: the forests contain bear, wolverine, elk and lynx. The elk, once thought to be almost extinct, has reproduced so effectively that around 50,000 animals now have to be shot annually. Wild reindeer have mostly disappeared, and the ones still surviving in the north have been domesticated; there are currently around 200,000 in Finland.

The islands along the coast are home to vast numbers of seabirds, especially the Arctic tern and the black-backed

The Bean Goose
Mooring on the Oulunjärvi river

An Arctic fox

gull, and several species of waterfowl can be found in and around the inland lakes. There are also numerous species of fish in Finland which include salmon, pike and trout, the very popular whitefish *(siika)*, as well as the Baltic herring *(silakka)*.

Midnight sunset

The Midnight Sun and the Northern Lights

It's impossible to appreciate the Midnight Sun fully unless you've actually lived through an entire Finnish winter beforehand. During June and July, when day and night are separated by only a brief period of twilight in the south and the sun never sets in the far north, nature quickly makes up for what it has missed during the winter months. This time of the year has a special atmosphere all of its own that is enhanced by the flickering bonfires seen on the banks of rivers and islands which, according to Finnish superstition, ensure a good autumn harvest.

Kaamos is the Finnish name for the long polar night, when the sun remains below the horizon and the moon and stars reflect in the snow to create a twilight of their own.

The northern lights *(aurora borealis)* are a fascinating natural phenomenon. The Same thought they were produced by the spirits of the dead; today we know they are caused by the interaction of positively charged particles (protons and electrons) from outside the atmosphere with atoms of the earth's upper atmosphere. The ions emit radiation at various wavelengths, thus creating the characteristic colours of the aurora (red and greenish blue). Science aside, it's a stunning spectacle to observe.

Reindeer

The semi-domesticated reindeer has always represented much more than a meal on four legs. Its skin contributes to bedding, and antlers and bones provide raw materials

Herding reindeer

12

for tools and utensils. Until the introduction of the motorised skidoo, it also provided a major means of transport. Reindeer herding has existed in Finland since the 17th century, though if legends are to be believed, the Same were herding the animals over 2,000 years ago. The Same language contains several hundred words used only for reindeer to describe the gender, age, antlers, colour, length, thickness of fur and even the animal's shape of head.

The nuclear reactor disaster at Chernobyl in the Ukraine in 1986 caused a minor economic catastrophe and widespread unemployment in Scandinavia when it became clear that the reindeer meat had become contaminated by fall-out, but Finland's herds remained unharmed. Same craft products are no longer exclusively reindeer-based: several craftsmen also work with wood and silver (genuine Same craft articles bear the label Sami Duodi).

The Sauna

Probably the most well-known word in the Finnish language is sauna. The earliest saunas, in use about 2,000 years ago, were nothing more than primitive holes in the ground. These were followed by 'smoke saunas' in enclosed rooms or huts, later equipped with handy chimneys. The basic features of the sauna – warming up, perspiring, washing, cooling down – have not changed for centuries, despite the fact that electronically-controlled thermostats have replaced wood-fired ovens.

Siblings in a sauna

Nevertheless, several misconceptions about what a sauna actually involves still persist among non-Finns. Apart from seeing the name sauna being wrongly applied to all sorts of sweat-inducing constructions and devices, the Finns are particularly concerned about the increasingly sleazy reputation that the sauna has acquired abroad. The sauna has nothing to do with sexual *laisser faire* – men and women don't even bathe together unless they're from the same family. It is not a good way of losing weight either because after a sauna the body simply replaces whatever it loses. The idea that being invited into the sauna is a special honour for guests also has to be laid to rest.

Birch improves circulation

So what does a sauna involve? First of all you shower and check the air temperature (80–100°C). As things get warmer, the humidity can be regulated by pouring water regularly on to the stove. This hot phase is then followed by a cooling-off period. Then the whole procedure is repeated. A piece of birch is useful for improving circulation, and a towel is useful for steam and heat circulation around the head. After the final cold shower, the best thing to do is just relax. A sauna not only opens the pores, it opens the soul, too. Every Finn's dream is to own a summer-house beside a lake where, still steaming from the sauna, they can jump directly into the cold water.

Historical Highlights

8000BC Tribes from eastern Europe – the ancestors of today's Same (Lapps) – settle the Finnish Arctic coast. They hunt bear and reindeer.

1800–1600BC The Central European 'Boat Axe' culture arrives from the east. Trade with Sweden begins from Bronze Age settlements along the Finnish west coast.

AD100 Tacitus describes the Fenni in *Germania*, probably referring to Finland's original inhabitants, the Same.

c 400 The 'Baltic Finns', or Suomalaiset, cross the Baltic and settle in Finland, gradually absorbing the Same population. Sweden's influence over its 'eastern province' begins, although the migrants embark on an isolated existence, living in clans and cut off from mainstream European developments.

1155 Impatient with the nuisance and danger posed by pagan Finnish clans raiding the Christian people of southern Sweden, King Erik of Sweden launches a crusade into Finland; further Swedish invasions take place in 1239 and 1293, subjugating large areas of the country.

1323 The Treaty of Shlisselburg establishes the official border between Sweden and Novgorod. It runs from St Petersburg northwestwards through the lake region to the Gulf of Bothnia.

1362 Finland becomes a province of Sweden.

1523 Gustav Vasa (1523–60) ascends the Swedish throne. The Reformation passes through Finland without bloodshed. The Lutheran faith is introduced from Germany by Mikael Agricola (1510–57), a bishop of Turku, whose translation of the Bible forms the basis of the Finnish literary language.

1595 The 25-year war with Russia is concluded by the Treaty of Teusina; the eastern border now extends as far as the Arctic coast, allowing Finns to live in the far north.

1617 The Peace of Stolbovo. Russia cedes Ingermanland and part of Karelia to the kingdom of Sweden-Finland.

1640 First university is established in Turku.

1696 One third of the population dies after a disastrous harvest. Sweden offers no assistance.

1700 Peter the Great occupies the Neva river and moves into Karelian isthmus.

1714–21 The 'Great Wrath'. Russia attacks Sweden and occupies Finland. Under the Treaty of Uusikaupunki in 1721, the tsar returns much of Finland but keeps Eastern Karelia.

1741 The 'Lesser Wrath'. Following Sweden's declaration of war, Russian troops occupy Finland again until the Treaty of Turku in 1743. The Russians cede a section of Finland back to Sweden, but move their border westwards.

1773 Attempts to gain independence from Sweden fail. A peasant uprising results in reforms.

1807 Tsar Alexander I attacks and occupies Finland in an attempt to force Sweden to join Napoleon's economic blockade. The Treaty of Hamina cedes all of the country to Russia.

1809 The tsar guarantees the Finns beneficial terms at the Porvoo Diet. Finland becomes an autonomous Russian grand duchy.

1812 Because of Turku's proximity to Sweden, Alexander I shifts the capital to Helsinki. Finnish Karelia ('old Finland') joins rest of the country.

1863 Differences of opinion between the Swedish-speaking ruling class and the Finnish nationalists are resolved, finally giving Finnish-speakers equal status.

1899 Tsar Nicholas II draws up the 'February Manifesto'; Russification process fuels flames of Finnish resistance. Sibelius writes *Finlandia* but is forced to publish it as 'Opus 26, No 7'.

1905 Russia is defeated by Japan, and the general strike in Moscow spreads to Finland. Finland regains a measure of autonomy.

1906 Finnish women become the first in Europe to be given the vote.

1908–14 Tsar Nicholas II reinstates the Russification programme and removes the new parliament's powers; any laws passed in Finland still have to be ratified by the tsar.

1915 Finnish volunteers join the tsar's army.

1917 The October Revolution in Russia. Finland declares its independence from the new Soviet Union. The senate elects PE Svinhufvud as its first president. The new state is officially recognised by Russia, France and Scandinavia.

1918 A radical wing of the Social Democratic Party tries to introduce a Russian-style revolution, plunging Finland into a Civil War. The 'Red Guard' fights the 'White Guard'. The latter, right-wing government troops with German military support under the leadership of General Mannerheim, finally defeat the 'Red Guard'.

1918–19 Friedrich Karl, Prince of Hessen, is offered the throne of Finland but declines. On 17 July 1919 the Republic of Finland comes into being under President KJ Ståhlberg (1919–25).

1920 Treaty of Tartu defines the border between Soviet Russia and newly independent Finland and settles ongoing issues of independence or autonomy of East Karelia.

1922 The Åland Islands are granted autonomy.

1939–40 Stalin's attempts to occupy all Finland spark off the so-called 'Winter War' between Finland and the Soviet Union. Finland successfully defends itself. Under the Treaty of Moscow in 1940, Finland is forced to surrender 11 percent of its territory to the Soviet Union.

1941–4 Finland clings to its neutrality, but out of the fear of a Soviet invasion is drawn closer to Nazi Germany. Hitler begins his Russian campaign, and the 'Continuation War' breaks out between Finland and the Soviet Union. Britain, allied with Russia, declares war on Finland in December 1941.

The German defeat at Stalingrad in 1943 results in the signing of a peace treaty between Finland and the Soviet Union in 1944. Finland is forced to give up the Petsamo region, and the border is restored to its 1940 position. War reparations are severe, and Finland is also compelled to drive the remaining Germans from its territory.

The retreating German army destroys many towns in Lapland.

1947 The peace treaty signed in Paris on 10 February reiterates the conditions of the armistice.

1948 Under the leadership of Paasikivi, the Treaty of Friendship, Co-operation and Mutual Assistance (FCMA) is signed, laying the foundations for long-term neighbourly relations with the Soviet Union.

1952 Russian fears are aroused when Finland joins in the formation of the Nordic Council. Helsinki hosts the Olympic Summer Games, adding fuel to the fire.

1955 Finland is admitted to the United Nations.

1956–81 President Urho Kekkonen maintains good policy relations with the Soviet Union.

1969 Preparations begin for the European Security Conference in Helsinki.

1972 The Strategic Arms Limitation Talks (SALT) are held in Helsinki.

1975 The Helsinki Accords are signed as part of the Conference on Security and Cooperation in Europe (CSCE).

1982 The Social Democrat Mauno Koivisto succeeds Kekkonen.

1990 The Finnish government declares several sections of the Paris Treaty of 1947 to be no longer applicable.

1991 The treaty of Friendship, Co-operation and Mutual Assistance (FCMA) with the former Soviet Union is replaced by a treaty emphasising good neighbourliness and cooperation.

1992 Finland applies to join the European Union.

1995 Finland joins the EU.

2000 The Social Democrat Tarja Halonen is the first elected female president.

2002 Finland becomes the first country in Northern Europe to adopt euro coins and bank notes.

Helsinki

1. Senate Square
2. Havis Amanda
3. Grönqvist House
4. State Council Banqueting Hall
5. Helsingin Sanomat museum
6. Sinebrychoff Brewery
7. Old Russian Garrison Theatre
8. Old Church
9. Town Hall
10. Presidential Palace
11. Art Nouveau Pharmacy
12. Eol Building
13. Katajanokka Casino
14. Olofsburg
15. Wanha Satama
16. Marine Hotel and Congress Centre

The Three Blacksmiths, Helsinki

Preceding pages: Hikers on Ukko-Koli

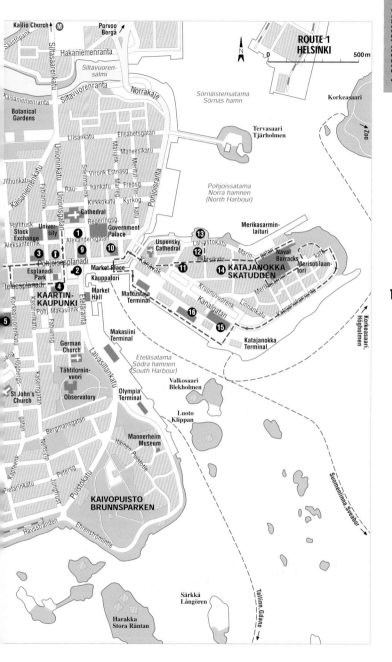

Route 1

Helsinki – Daughter of the Baltic

Helsinki enjoys a brief summer

Helsinki (pop. 560,000, www.hel.fi/tourism) is similar to many major cities of Eastern Europe both in appearance and in mood, having been an outpost of Tsarist Russia for many years. However, Finland's own late 19th-century National Romantic style is also reflected in its harmonious architecture. The city is full of street entertainment during the brief summer, and has a very lively nightlife. Most of Helsinki's sights are within walking distance of each other.

History

Helsinki was founded north of the mouth of the River Vantaa in 1550 by the Swedish king Gustav Vasa to compete with Tallinn, whose port was controlled by the Hanseatic League. In 1640 the city was shifted slightly southwards along the coast, but its fortunes subsequently declined as it battled against the Great Famine (1697), the Great Northern War (1700–21) and The Great Plague (1710). The fire of 1808 reduced Helsinki to ashes.

In 1746 the Swedes ensured Helsinki's importance by building Suomenlinna Fortress. Three years after they ceded Finland to Russia (1809) Tsar Alexander I raised Helsinki to the status of capital in place of Turku/Åbo. In 1816 Alexander commissioned the architect Carl Ludwig Engel to completely rebuild the city. Engel designed the city in the neoclassical style, lining its wide streets with Empire-style brick buildings. In 1828, the University of Turku moved to Helsinki. When it was made Finland's capital, Helsinki had a population of 4,000; today, one million live and work in Greater Helsinki, which has become an important metropolis of industry, trade and culture.

Sights

The two city walks in this guide explore the highlights that can easily be reached from the ferry docks in the southern harbour. Those visitors eager to venture further should take the tram route described.

Noble Helsinki

Helsinki's ★★★ **Senate Square (Senaatintori)** ❶ is situated 100 metres away from the market in the south harbour. It bears Engel's unmistakeable neoclassical stamp, and its architectural harmony has made it the finest square in the city.

The Cathedral

Senate Square is dominated by the ★ **Cathedral**, reached by an impressive flight of granite steps. Begun by Engel, the cathedral was given its gilt domes and the *Twelve Apostles* by another Prussian architect, Ernst Lohrmann; their rounded contours contrast with the brilliant white clarity of the building as a whole. The ascetic Lutheran interior contains three striking statues of Luther, Melanchthon and Mikael Agricola.

The **Government Palace** (Valtioneuvosto) on the eastern side of the square is one of Engel's most important works, built in 1822 to house the Senate. It was here that the Finn Eugen Schauman assassinated the unpopular Russian governor-general Nikolai Bobrikov in 1904. The assassination resulted in a general strike and the reintroduction of autonomy, followed in 1906 by women's suffrage and the creation of a modern parliament.

The University

Opposite the Government Palace, on the eastern side of the square, are the Ionic columns of **Helsinki University** (Yliopisto). It was designed by Engel as a private residence for the Tsarist governor-general; the University was moved here in 1827 after the building in Turku was destroyed by fire. Engel gave the neighbouring **University Library** building a magnificent facade.

At the centre of the square is the statue of **Tsar Alexander II** (1863); he introduced a separate currency for Finland (the markka) and made Finnish the national language. The statue of Alexander with his arm outstretched in the direction of the harbour, and the cathedral in the background, is Helsinki's most popular photo subject. The section of the square towards the harbour is lined by 18th-century merchants' buildings, with shops and cafés on the ground floors. The boutiques in the **Kiselev House** (on the corner of Unioninkatu), which once belonged to the Stockmann department store, are particularly good. The **Sederholm House** (on the corner of Katariinankatu) was built in 1757, and is the oldest stone structure in Helsinki.

Tsar Alexander – a popular image

Opposite the statue of Alexander II is the Esplanadi Park, with the famous boulevard known as ★★ **Esplanadi**

Shade in the Esplanade

Enjoy the view from the Savoy

(or Espa as it is generally called), the most popular promenade in the city. It was also laid out by Engel, in 1812, and its elegance is timeless.

The Espa consists of two broad parallel streets: the Northern Esplanade (Pohjoisesplanadi) and the Southern Esplanade (Eteläesplanadi), extending from the market along to the Mannerheimintie. Ville Valgren's well-proportioned **Havis Amanda ❷**, the bronze maiden up on the fountain at the east end of the strip of parkland, raised several eyebrows when she first appeared here in 1908. On 1 May each year, when Finland's students take their exams, she can be seen wearing a student's white cap. The outdoor terrace of the **Kappeli Café-Restaurant** provides a good view of the **Espa's Open-Air Stage** (weekdays 5 and 6.30pm, weekends noon and 1.30pm), where musical performances are held every summer.

To the right of the stage, at No 19 Pohjoiseplanadi, is the **Helsinki Municipal Tourist Office**. One cross-street further to the west, the **Grönqvist House** (Grönqvistin talo) ❸ extends from the Fabianinkatu as far as the Kluuvikatu. This was Scandinavia's largest private apartment building when it was completed in 1883. Directly opposite is the oldest building on the Esplanadi, an Empire building with a balcony. This houses the **State Council Banqueting Hall** (Valtioneuvoston juhlahuoneisto) ❹. The building is known as the 'Smolna' for short; the nickname is a reference to Leningrad's Smolny Institute, the seat of the Bolsheviks, and is a reminder of the time when Helsinki was occupied by the Red Guard during the Civil War in 1918.

The **Statue of JL Runeberg** at the centre of the park is a work by the son of the national poet, Walter Runeberg, and was completed in 1885. A striking feature of the South Esplanade here is the ★★ **Savoy Restaurant** with its interior designed by Aino and Alvar Aalto; there's also a superb view across the centre of the city from its rooftop terrace. The matching facade on the Northern Esplanade opposite is occupied by the 5-star Hotel Kämp, where Sibelius and other artists once resided. There are several very valuable paintings in the banking hall, which is modelled after the banqueting hall. Today, several famous shops along the Northern Esplanade specialise in Finnish design products. At the western end of the Northern Esplanade is the ★ **Academic Bookstore** (on the corner of Keskuskatu), one of the largest bookshops in Europe. The striking horseshoe-shaped **Swedish Theatre**, Finland's most famous Swedish-speaking theatre, rounds off the Espa nicely.

From the Espa, stroll off in a westerly direction towards Erottajankatu. The first street off to the left, Ludviginkatu (named after Carl Ludwig Engel), contains the newspaper

museum in the former editorial building of the daily paper *Helsingin Sanomat* ❺. Beyond them, past the many shops in the pedestrian precincts in **Iso Roobertinkatu** and **Fredrikinkatu**, is the magnificent avenue **Bulevardi** with its highly ornate facades. The red-brick building on the corner of Hietalahdenranta and Bulevardi contains the former **Sinebrychoff Brewery** ❻ – the oldest in Finland – and its founder's **Museum of Art** (Monday, Thursday, Friday 9am–6pm, Wednesday 9am–8pm, Saturday and Sunday 11am–5pm). Luxury cruise liners and icebreakers – both of them highly successful Finnish export articles – are constructed at the enormous harbour shipyard nearby.

At the **Hietalahti** marketplace (flea market: daily from 8am, also summer evenings), turn back along the north side of Bulevardi. The **old Russian garrison theatre** ❼ with its reddish decoration contained the Finnish National Opera until 1993. Nestling in a green square is the **Old Church** ❽, the first Lutheran church in the young capital, constructed according to Engel's plans in 1826.

The Kalevankatu leads to the **Three Blacksmiths Monument**, a popular meeting-place in summer and forming a transition to Helsinki's busiest shopping mile, the **Aleksanterinkatu**, with its crowds and buskers. There is an ever increasing number of cafés, restaurants and night spots in the area, as well as countless bars. At the 'Zetor' beer is served in litre-sized mugs. And don't forget those typically Finnish dancing venues which are already in full swing by early afternoon.

It's well worth paying at least a brief visit to the famous ★★**Stockmann**, the largest department store in the whole of Scandinavia. Beyond it is the oldest modern glass-covered shopping arcade in Finland, the **Rautatalo**, designed by Alvar Aalto, with its marble inner courtyard, fountain, restaurants and shops.

Bulevardi

The head of Christ in the Museum of Art

23

The Old Church

One attraction of the Zetor

The Keskuskatu opens out at the square in front of the ★★ **Railway Station** (1916). Eliel Saarinen's building is regarded as a National Romantic masterpiece. It is rather reminiscent of an enormous old radio, and the pompous-looking muscular men on its facade seem to be admiring its controls.

The ★★ **Ateneum**, south of the railway station on the Kaivokatu, is the most important museum of late 19th- and 20th-century art in Finland; it contains masterpieces dating from the Golden Age of Finnish painting by artists such as Akseli Gallen-Kallela. Outside the entrance of the nearby **National Theatre** *(Suomen Kansallisteatteri)*, home of Finnish drama since 1872, is Wäino Aaltonen's statue of Aleksis Kivi, Finland's first playwright.

A tram ride through Helsinki

The Mannerheimintie

Inside the Rock Church

This tour involves boarding a No 3T tram outside the Cathedral. South of the **Main Post Office**, with the large equestrian statue of Mannerheim outside it, the tram route crosses the **Mannerheimintie**, the longest street in Helsinki. On its western side (note: the 3T tram doesn't travel along it) to the north is the **Parliament Building** (Eduskuntatalo) and the **National Museum** (Tuesday and Wednesday, 11am–8pm, Thursday to Sunday 11am–6pm). This museum documents the history of Finland from prehistoric times to the present day, and is housed in a National Romantic style building designed in 1902 by Lindgren, Gesellius and Saarinen; the foyer contains some fine Kalevala motifs by Akseli Gallen-Kallela. Directly opposite is Helsinki's **Municipal Museum** in the little Villa Hankasalmi (Wednesday to Sunday, 11am–5pm) and also Alvar Aalto's **Finlandia Hall** (Finlandiatalo), a concert hall and congress centre (guided tours available); it was completed in 1975, and in the same year the CSCE conference was held there *(see page 15)*.

The tram route loops around through the suburb of Töölö. Here it's worth stopping at the ★ **Rock Church** (Temppeliaukion kirkko). This fantastic vision of a round church was realised in 1969 by Timo and Tuomio Suomalainen. The interior was blown out of a piece of solid rock 12m (39ft) above street level; the walls were left bare and the whole is vaulted by a copper wire dome.

Five hundred metres (¼ mile) to the west of the church is the famous **Hietaniemi Cemetery**. This cemetery is the last resting-place of many well-known Finns, including CL Engel and Marshal Mannerheim, as well as victims of World War II.

A 1-km (½-mile) stroll to the north of the cemetery leads to Sibelius Park, containing the ★ **Sibelius Monument**,

Eila Hiltunen's abstract steel construction which resembles a weird organ.

The 3T crosses the Mannerheimintie once again near a new building on the banks of the Töölönlahti, the **National Opera**, which was designed by Hyväniemi, Karhunen and Parkkinen and completed in 1993. The **Olympic Stadium** can already be seen behind the trees; it was built for the 1940 Games, but because of World War II they were not held here until 1952. The observation platform up on its 72-m (236-ft) high tower provides an excellent panoramic view. There is also a **Sports Museum** nearby (Urheilumuseo, Monday to Friday 11am–5pm, Saturday and Sunday noon–4pm).

The 3T tram now heads for the **Linnanmäki Amusement Park** (May to August, noon–10pm), where there's a roller coaster as well as several dance halls and restaurants. Further on along the tram route, at the northern end of Siltasaarenkatu, another of Helsinki's major sights awaits: the **Church of Kallio**, a National Romantic structure with a fine tower.

The **Hesperia Park** is a green oasis extending the length of the western shore of the Töölönlahti. Timo Penttilä's Municipal Theatre, partly hewn out of the rock, was built on the eastern bank in 1967.

25

Maritime Helsinki

The life of maritime Helsinki has always revolved around the ★ **market place** (Kauppatori) which is usually very busy, especially during the summer. Early morning is the best time to come here, when crates of fruit and vegetables get piled up and the **market hall** opens its doors – the building dates from Tsarist times. The market café is a popular place for a quick coffee on the way to work, and small stalls in the **Colera harbour basin** sell freshly-caught fish. In the mornings the market square, with the neoclassical obelisk at its centre – known familiarly as 'the toothpick' – gradually fills up.

The neoclassical **Town Hall** (Kaupungintalo) ❾ at the northwestern corner was added by Engel in 1833, and was originally planned as a hotel; in 1843 he turned a rich merchant's house two blocks further away into the **Presidential Palace** ❿. It's only a palace in name these days, though: the president lives and works in **Mäntyniemi** in the Meilahti district of the city.

To the east, and set back slightly, is the **Main Guardhouse** (changing of the guard daily, parades at 1pm on Tuesday and Friday).

The route now continues over the canal bridge to the **Katajanokka** peninsula. This is the former location of all

Vegetable stalls and the old market hall

The guard changes daily

Uspensky Cathedral

Doorway on the Luotsikatu

Harbour view

the run-down, ramshackle wooden huts which made Helsinki quite a notorious place until the late 19th century. The eye-catching gold-red-and-blue ★ **Uspensky Cathedral** (May to September, Tuesday to Saturday 9.30am–4pm, Monday 9.30am–4pm, Sunday noon–3pm; otherwise Tuesday to Saturday 9.30am–4pm, Sunday noon–3pm, Monday closed) can be seen next to the water; it was designed in 1868 by AM Gornostayev, and the vault inside the rather dark interior is supported by four granite columns.

The Katajanokka quarter of the city has undergone a process of 'yuppification' in recent years: several of the old red granaries and warehouses here have been converted into restaurants and boutiques. The walk continues now along the **Luotsikatu** where there are a number of art nouveau houses. The finest structure here is a residential building with highly decorative doors. It was designed in 1897 by the architectural office of Gesellius & Partners. The building on the corner of Kruunuvuorenkatu, recognised by its decorative owls, foxes and squirrels, contains a fine **art nouveau pharmacy** ⓫.

At the junction of Luotsikatu and Katajanokankatu on the left is the striking **Eol Building** ⓬ (1901, Gesellius & Partners), and next to the water is the **Katajanokka Casino** ⓭; on the right the representative residential area of **Olofsburg** ⓮ can be seen, and further eastwards is the Northern Harbour, where Finland's icebreaker fleet is moored, ready for winter action.

A flight of steps descends via a small gate to Engel's **Naval Barracks**, in military use until 1968. Walk further now via Merisotilaantori Square and the beach promenade to the **Katajanokka Terminal**. The nearby **Wanha Satama** roofed-over shopping arcade ⓯, with its restaurants and exhibition rooms, was built on the site of several

old warehouses. The **Marina Hotel and Congress Centre** here is where the CSCE conference was held in 1992. The art nouveau hall of the main customs office is an architectural masterpiece; the customs building marks the end of this short tour.

The Customs House

Not far from the Swedish ferry docks at the other side of the South Harbour in the district of **Kaivopuisto**, the **Mannerheim Museum** (Friday to Sunday 11am–4pm) documents the life of its former occupant. Nearby, the 30m (100ft) high observatory hill can be seen with the **Astronomical Observatory** on the top, which was designed by Engel; at the foot of the hill is the red-brick German-Lutheran church. The oldest yacht club in Finland is located on the island of Valkosaari opposite.

Järvenpää

Järvenpää is 38km (24 miles) north of Helsinki and getting there by bus or train is easy. The reason it is so famous is because it was here that the composer Jean Sibelius lived from 1904 onwards with his wife Aino (sister of the artist Eero Järnefelt), in the house he named after her called ★★ **Ainola**. This excursion is a must for all Sibelius fans: the house is in a very calm setting, close to lakes and forests, and the interior is plainly but elegantly furnished. The composer is buried in the grounds; the plain gravestone is inscribed simply with his name.

For those unfamiliar with Sibelius's music, two very good works to accompany any trip to Finland are *Finlandia* (originally published as *Opus 26, No 7* in 1899, after the Russians complained about its patriotic sentiment) and the equally famous *Karelia Suite*.

Suomenlinna and Korkeasaari islands

Boats for the island excursions leave from Kauppatori.

Boats leave from Kauppatori

★★ **Suomenlinna.** In order to protect what remained of their Finnish territory, between 1748 and 1772 the Swedes built fortifications on this group of five islands off Helsinki. The natural beauty of the landscape attracts picnickers, museum visitors, artists and sun worshippers. Small cafés, a restaurant, museums, the bathing resort island of Pihlajasaari and the Seurasaari Municipal Park all provide a varied day's programme.

★ **Korkeasaari.** This island has been a popular excursion destination since the year 1888, when it built its zoo. While the zoo – which specialises in 'cold climate' animals – may not be one of the world's greatest, the beaches of Korkeasaari and the superb views are worth the trip in themselves.

Ice-cream Sunday

Turku is on the River Aura

Route 2

Turku – more than just a transit city

It's a sad fact that most people come to Turku only because it happens to be the place where ferries dock: many rush on to their destination unaware of what the city itself has to offer. Turku (also known by its Swedish name of Åbo) is much more than Finland's third-largest urban centre (pop. 174,000, www.turkutouring.fi). It's the oldest city in the country, home of the first university, and the capital for a full five centuries before giving up the role to Helsinki in 1812, due to its uncomfortable proximity to Sweden. Despite its size, it is certainly the most interesting town in the country after Helsinki.

The stroll around the city described here takes around two hours (not including visiting times at sights) and covers a distance of 4km (3 miles); it follows the course of the Aura river where many of Turku's main sights are located, but also takes in the castle and the cathedral, the two symbols of the town's important past.

Sights

The Cathedral

Turku's ★★ **Cathedral** was built on the site of a small wooden chapel erected in 1229 when Turku was the first bishopric in Finland, and is the country's most important medieval structure (mid-April to mid-September Monday to Friday 10am–6pm, Saturday 10am–3pm, Sunday after mass; otherwise Monday to Saturday 10am–3pm, Sunday after mass). Originally consecrated in 1300, the Cathedral has been continually restored, altered and renovated over the centuries. The side-aisles were added during medieval times. Despite the many different architectural styles, the main impression one gets is Late Romantic. The bell-tower was added in the 19th century; its bells toll 20 times each Christmas Eve, according to an ancient Scandinavian tradition which today is practised only in Turku. The cathedral contains the tombs of several famous Finns. A simple sarcophagus of black marble holds the mortal remains of Catharine Månsdotter, a flower-girl from Turku who married King Erik XIV of Sweden in 1568; a statue on the southern wall of the cathedral stands in memory of the reformer Mikael Agricola; and the incredibly ornate coffin of Torsten Stålhandske, a Finnish cavalry commander who won several victories during the Thirty Years' War, stands opposite the graves of Patrick Ogilvie and Samuel Cockburn, two Scots who fought at his side.

Resting place of famous Finns

Not far away from the cathedral, the **University**, first proposed in 1640 by Sweden's Queen Christina, proves how cleverly the Swedes succeeded in integrating the local upper class. The founder of the university, **Per Brahe**, has a special park in the cathedral grounds named after him; he was Swedish governor-general of Finland on two occasions. Also not far from the cathedral is the **Sibelius Museum** at Piispankatu 17 (Tuesday to Sunday 11am–4pm, Wednesdays also 6–8pm). Sibelius had no direct connection with Turku but at the small concert hall here, recorded and sometimes even live performances of the

Sibelius

29

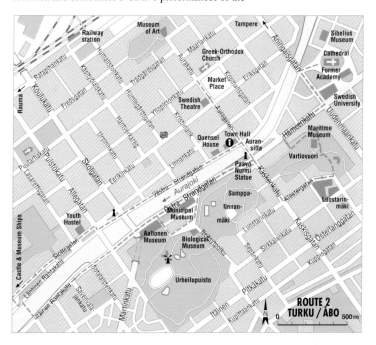

great man's works can often be heard. A little further away is the **Burgher's House Museum** (Ett Hem) at Piis-pankatu 14 (2 May to 30 September Tuesday to Sunday noon–3pm).

The most difficult 20 years in Turku's history began in 1809, when Sweden was forced to cede Finland to Russia. Three years later Tsar Alexander I shifted the seat of government and administration to Helsinki. Then in the autumn of 1827 the whole of Turku was destroyed by a fire apart from the Luoastarinmäki section of the city, which was situated slightly higher up. The new Turku was designed by CL Engel.

Walk along the River Aura as far as the Vartoivuori Hill with the **observatory** on top, built by Engel in 1819. It houses temporarily the **Turku Art Museum** which is being renovated. There's a good detour from here to old Turku and to the fascinating **Luostarinmäki Handicraft Museum** (16 April to 15 September 10am–6pm; otherwise, Tuesday to Sunday 10am–3pm), where 30 different workshops have exhibitions of traditional craft. The appearance of Turku is sharply defined by the Aura river, or Aurajoki, with the castle and the ferry harbour at its mouth. Swedish crusaders were soon followed here by merchants from far and wide who traded with the local population. The town thus grew spontaneously, and never needed to be artificially created like several others. Its year of foundation, 1229, was when Pope Gregory IX elevated Turku to the status of a bishopric.

30

Tempting cherries at the market

Another important role in the town's development was played by the German Hanseatic League (Turku had 13 German mayors between 1310 and 1471), and the glass-roofed Hansa Shopping Centre on the western side of the market-place is named after this period of civic history. Don't miss a stroll through Turku's **covered market** (open Monday to Saturday, and in the evening as well during the summertime); the old Slavonic word *turku* does actually mean 'market' (Finnish: *kauppatori*). The small stalls stretch along the entire length, with tempting arrays of *munkki*, a sort of doughnut, and *pulla*, a cake-like bread. Enjoy the delicious strawberries, a coffee in an original market café, and the splendid view of the Swedish Theatre and the Greek Orthodox Church.

The route from the market place to the west bank of the river leads past the pretty 18th-century **Quensel House** (Quenselin talo), which once belonged to a wealthy merchant who bought the plot as early as 1695 and is one of the few houses in Turku to have survived the devastating fire; today it contains the atmospheric **Apothecary Museum** (16 April to 15 September 10am–6pm, otherwise Tuesday to Sunday 10am–3pm).

Anyone weary of strolling at this point can board a

In the Apothecary Museum

The ferry is free

water-bus or the *Ukkopekka*, the last steamer in operation in Finland, and set off to explore Turku's myriad small islands. Landlubbers should visit one of the 10 restaurant-ships moored along the Aurajoki here. A little further downriver, the town ferry, or *Föri*, transports pedestrians and cyclists across the river free of charge. Since there's no limit on the number of trips you can take, this is a very good place for using a video camera. Anchored at the east bank of the river, is the sailing ship *Suomen Joutsen* (The Finnish Swan, open 15 May to 15 August noon–8pm). A navy training vessel during the 1930s, it was later a school ship for the Finnish trade fleet. On the west bank, near the castle, is the Swedish museum ship, *Sigyn*, launched in 1887 and recently renovated. Near the castle **Forum Marinum** is a modern maritime museum with exhibitions and ticket sales for the museum ships. The old mine-ship *Keihässalmi* can also be visited.

Sigyn museum ship

Before returning upriver along the east bank at this point, it's a good idea to pay a brief visit to Turku's **castle**, which dates back to 1280. Originally the stronghold of the royal Swedish governor, the castle received most of its main fortifications during the 16th century, when King Gustav Vasa made his son Johan the first duke of Finland. The castle was badly damaged during air raids in 1941, and restoration work took 15 years to complete. Today the Renaissance-style 'Duke Johan Castle Festival' in August and September includes splendid six-course banquets (delicious but very expensive); the food can be eaten with a knife, or with fingers for authenticity.

The castle dates back to 1280

The route back ends up at the Museum Park and the **Wäinö Aaltonen Museum** (Itäinen Rantakatu 38, Tuesday to Sunday 11am–7pm), where works by one of Finland's most important sculptors, Wäinö Aaltonen (1894–1966), may be admired. The nearby **Biological Museum** features several exhibitions documenting the country's fauna and flora (16 April to 15 September 10am–6pm, 16 September–15 April Tuesday to Sunday 10am–3pm).

In the park itself, on Samppalina Hill, the last windmill in Turku can be seen, and right next to it is a running track once graced by the top Finnish athlete Paavo Nurmi (1897–1973). Claimed to be the greatest long-distance runner of all time, he took part in three Olympic competitions and won 9 gold and three silver medals, setting 31 world records in the process. This stroll ends at the **Paavo Nurmi Statue** on the Auransilta Bridge.

Despite its size, Turku is a very sociable place, and the prosperous years under Swedish rule combined with a high student population from its two universities not only make it one of the most culturally interesting towns in Finland but also explain why the nightlife here is so good.

Paavo Nurmi smashed all records

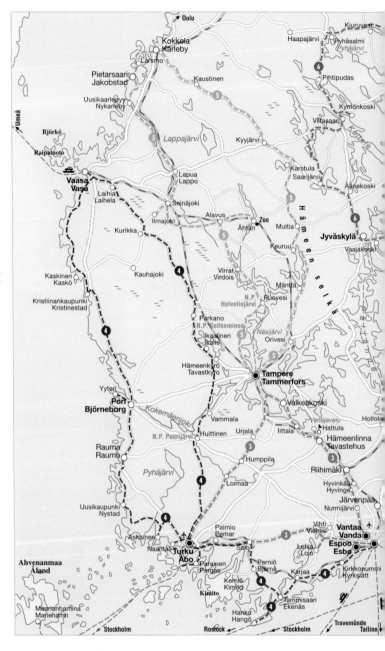

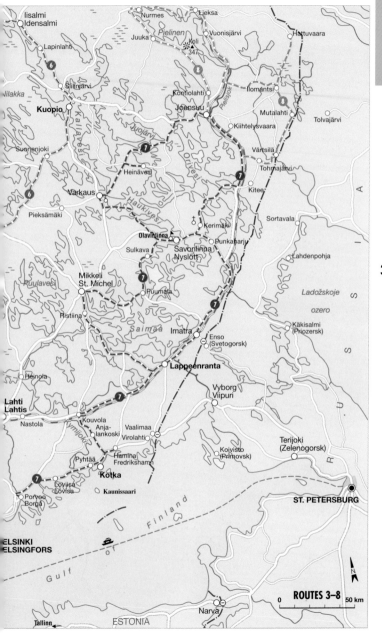

Iisalmi
Idensalmi
Nurmes
Lieksa
Pielinen
Juuka
Koli
347
Vuonisjärvi
Hattuvaara
Lapinlahti
6
8
Siilinjärvi
Kontiolahti
Ilomantsi
8
Kuopio
Joensuu
Mutalahti
Tolvajärvi
Nilakka
Kiihtelysvaara
Suonenjoki
7
Värtsilä
Heinävesi
Tohmajärvi
Varkaus
7
Kitee
Pieksämäki
Kerimäki
Sortavala
Olavinlinna
Sulkava
Savonlinna
Nyslott
Punkaharju
Lahdenpohja
Mikkeli
St. Michel
7
Puumala
Ladožskoje
ozero
Ristiina
Saimaa
Käkisalmi
(Priozersk)
Imatra
7
Enso
(Svetogorsk)
Heinola
Lappeenranta
Vyborg
Viipuri
Lahti
Lahtis
7
Nastola
Kouvola
Anja-
lankoski
Vaalimaa
Virolahti
Terijoki
(Zelenogorsk)
Koivisto
(Primovsk)
Pyhtää
Hamina
Fredrikshamn
7
Loviisa
Lovisa
Kotka
Porvoo
Borgå
Kaunissaari
ST. PETERSBURG
ELSINKI
ELSINGFORS
of
Finland
Gulf
N
Narva
ROUTES 3–8
0   50 km
Tallinn
ESTONIA

Route 3

The Glass Triangle *See map, pages 32–3*

Helsinki – Vantaa – Hyvinkää – Riihimäki – Hämeen-linna – Iittala – Valkeakoski – Sääksmäki – Tampere – Urjala – Loimaa – Turku – Salo – Lohja – Helsinki (500km/310 miles). *Note: mileage given beside a town name represents how far along the route it is.*

This round trip leads from Helsinki into the cultural heart of Finland: Häme or Tavastland. The triangle between Helsinki, Tampere and Turku is fascinating for its history, art and festivals, as well as for its many glass factories (with products on sale). The 500-km (310-mile) route is best done by car, but train connections are also possible (along the Helsinki–Tampere–Turku–Helsinki line).

Those leaving Helsinki by car along the E12 will pass the city's Vantaa Airport on their right. The **Heureka Science Centre** in **Vantaa** (pop. 180,000) has various fascinating exhibitions on natural science themes, and is entertaining for young and old (open all year, 10am–6pm, Thursdays to 8pm).

Just 15km (9 miles) away is **Nurmijärvi**, birthplace of writer Aleksis Kivi. The western foothills of the Salpausselkä range of mountains are a distinctive feature of the otherwise flat and featureless landscape near **Hyvinkää** (Hyvinge, pop. 42,000), 56km (34 miles), a town well known to train and architecture enthusiasts. Its **railway museum** (Hyvinkäänkatu 9, 1 June to 31 September daily 11am–6pm; 1 September to 31 October Tuesday to Saturday noon–3pm, Sunday noon–5pm; 1 November to 19 February Sunday noon–5pm; 20 February to 31 May Tues-

Hyvinkää is well known to train enthusiasts

day to Saturday noon–3pm, Sunday noon–5pm) is housed inside old railway buildings dating from 1870. Aarno Ruusuvori's triangular church here is very striking; it ushered in a new epoch of church building in the 1960s.

Finnish design contains several elements taken from the natural world; water is the most obvious theme when it comes to Finnish glassware. Ice is a very popular motif on structured glass articles, and it was the Finnish landscape with its many bays which inspired Alvar Aalto's famous 1930s vase. The **Glass Museum** (Tehtaankatu 23, May to August 10am–6pm, September to April Tuesday to Sunday 10am–6pm, closed January) in the town of **Riihimäki** (pop. 26,000), 68km (42 miles), documents the history of the Finnish glass industry and the sheer variety of this fascinating craft. Artists and craftsmen can also be seen at work in the nearby **Arts and Crafts Village**.

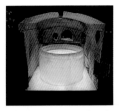
Glass museum in Riihimäki

Hämeenlinna (Tavastehus, pop. 46,400, www.hameenlinna.fi), 100km (62 miles), is named after its fortress, later used as a prison. The old **Hämeenlinna provincial prison** is also open to the public during the summer (1 June to 30 September Tuesday to Sunday 10am–5pm). Hugo Standertskjöld, a wealthy colonel, had the romantic **Aulanko** park laid out at the end of the 18th century; it has some fine ponds, pavilions and bowers. Apart from being Finland's oldest inland town, Hämeenlinna is probably most famous for being the birthplace of the country's most renowned composer, Jean Sibelius. The **Sibelius Birthplace** (May to August daily 10am–4pm, September to April noon–4pm) at Hallituskatu 11 has been reverently restored to how it looked during the first years of the composer's life .

Hämeenlinna castle

35

Aulanko Park

There's an unusual sight just beyond Hämeenlinna in the middle of a forest: the **Parola Tank Museum** (Parolannummi, May 9am–6pm, June to August 10am–7pm, September Saturday and Sunday 10am–4pm), with its 50 types of military tank from World War I and World War II. The Gothic frescoes in the 14th-century church of the Holy Cross in **Hattula** (10km/6 miles away from Hämeenlinna) make it one of the most interesting medieval buildings in Finland.

In **Iittala** (on the E12, a short distance after the turnoff to Kalvola), there is a fascinating **glass centre** (daily 10am–8pm, April to August 9am–8pm) where visitors can try blowing glass themselves; needless to say, the salesrooms are full of all kinds of excellent souvenirs, and keen bargain hunters can usually pick up flawed articles for next to nothing (the 'flaws' in this establishment are practically invisible).

Try some glass-blowing in Iittala

A popular subject for photographers near the paper and cellulose production centre of **Valkeakoski** (pop. 21,000),

Part of Tampere's industrial heritage

150km (90 miles), is the 205-m (672-ft) long **suspension bridge** spanning the narrow part of Lake Vanajavesi. Near the bridge in the suburb of Valkeakoski known as Sääksmäki is the **Visavuori Studio**, which once belonged to the sculptor Emil Wikström; today the studio has been turned into a museum. The 'Kari Pavilion' here also contains caricatures by the sculptor's equally artistic grandson, Kari Suomalainen.

The landscape between here and Tampere shows the modern, industrialised face of Finland; but soon the town of **Tampere** (Tammerfors, pop. 198,000, www.tampere.fi/matkailu) 185km (114 miles) from Helsinki, comes into view. Tampere was founded in around 1800 on a small promontory just 421m (460 yards) across between Lake Näsijärvi and Lake Pyhäjärvi. The town's economic growth began over a century ago when Tsar Alexander I abolished taxes on local trade, and James Finlayson, a Scot, opened a textile factory here. He was soon followed by others, and today Tampere is Finland's biggest manufacturing centre. The **Tammerkoski Rapids** at the centre of the town (18m/59ft height difference) are a very good place to go salmon fishing – and are also an important source of hydroelectric power for the town. Modern Tampere has a university, shopping centres such as **Koskikeskus**, **Tullintori** and **Kehräsaari** (boutiques and workshops inside a former factory), and also quite a few interesting-looking inhabitants, especially all the students in their blue uniforms who drink beer in the same pubs, visit the same theatres and live in the same part of town, Pispala, with its colourful houses on their green slope.

The best way to spend a day in Tampere is to take a stroll on both sides of the rapids. Start off with a trip to the town's dignified **Market Hall** (Hämeenkatu) and to the Verkaranta Arts and Crafts Centre (Verkatehtaankatu 2). The figures by Wäinö Aaltonen on the **Hämeensilta Bridge** are strikingly original, and the **Keskustori** (central square in front of the cathedral church) is particularly colourful during the Flower Festival in late July and early August.

As far as museums are concerned, Tampere has quite a few options: there's the **Haihara Doll Museum** (early April to late September, 11am–5pm) with 4,000 dolls from all over the world (Hatanpäänkuja 1, with a boat link to the town centre); the **Hatan-Vapriikki Museum Centre** (Tuesday to Sunday 10am–6pm, Wed 11am–8pm) with exhibitions from prehistory to modern art; and also the unusual **Lenin Museum** (Monday to Friday 9am–6pm, Saturday and Sunday 11am–6pm), with exhibits documenting Lenin's stays in Finland after the failed 1905 revolution – it was here in Tampere that he first met Stalin. Reserve quite a bit of time for a stroll through the **Workers' Mu-**

Time stands still in the Worker's Museum

Särkänniemi amusement park

The view from the tower

seum of **Amuri** or Amurin työläismuseokortteli (Makasiinikatu 12, Tuesday to Sunday 10am–6pm), too, where
around 30 houses have been preserved complete with
memorabilia relating to their former occupants. These
houses give a good idea of what life must have been like
in the latter years of the 19th century.

Families will certainly enjoy the **Särkänniemi Complex** (mid-April to September) with its 168m (551ft) high
Näsinneula observation tower – the highest in Finland
– and its revolving restaurant 124m (406ft) up. The complex also has a **dolphinarium**, **planetarium** and an
aquarium. Contemporary art can be admired in the **Sara
Hilden Museum** (daily 11am–6pm), situated very close
to the Särkänniemi Complex, and there's also a zoo nearby
with animals that don't mind being stroked – ideal for
young children.

The best time to appreciate Tampere's architecture is
probably late afternoon. The **Tampere Hall**, designed in
1990 by Esa Piiroinen and Sakari Aartelo, is a futuris-
tic-functional congress centre and concert hall. Light
streaming into the spectacular blue and white building
picks out the main lobby's fountains, which commemo-
rate the Tammerkoski rapids as the source of prosperity.
The main hall, which holds 2,000 people, is magnificent;
locals of Tampere are proud to point out that it is bigger
than Helsinki's Finlandia, and the acoustics are much better. There is also a small auditorium housing 500 people.

The **City Library**, also known locally as 'the turkey',
is a real jewel of contemporary architecture, and was designed in 1986 by Raili and Reima Pietilä. The **cathedral** (Tuomiokirkko) is made of bluish-grey granite, and
is a successful piece of Finnish National Romanticism;
it was designed by Lars Sonck. Magnus Enckell's mo-
saic windows are striking, but the most remarkable

Tampere Cathedral

feature of the cathedral is its symbolic frescoes by Hugo Simberg, extending a full 40m (131ft); some of them are very gory indeed. The enormous concrete **Kalevala Church** was also designed by Pietilä, in 1960. Its 30m (98ft) high interior is very striking.

There's quite a lot going on in Tampere during the evenings, especially in March (Film Festival), June (Pispalan Sottiisi Folklore Festival), August (Summer Theatre Festival) and November (Tampere Jazz Festival).

Now take road number 9 in the direction of Turku, passing seemingly endless fields and pastureland. Although there's only the odd stretch of forest visible, it's worth remembering that four-fifths of Finland is actually covered by it. The typically Finnish farms are separated by fields and are quite a distance apart.

Tampere's 'Finlandia Queen'

There are two more glass centres, in **Urjala** and 20km (12 miles) outside **Loimaa**: **Nuutajärvi** and **Humppila**. Nuutajärvi is Finland's oldest glass factory, and differs from Iittala in that coloured, Italian-style glass is also produced here. Cheap souvenirs can be bought here and at Humppila; the tools used by the glass-blowers can also be admired in the Glass Museum.

The coast near Turku features entirely different scenery. Unfortunately the austere beauty of the thousands of offshore islands and their cliffs here can only rarely be glimpsed from the mainland.

There are two alternative routes back to Helsinki from **Turku** *(see page 28)*, 340km (211 miles); those in a hurry can take the direct road via Salo. **Salo** (pop. 24,000), 390km (242 miles), contains a factory which has been manufacturing pharmaceutical glassware since 1920; architectural highlights include the **Uskela Church** designed by CL Engel in 1832 and the **Anchor Monument** in the marketplace. Further on, a slight detour will take you to **Lohja** (Lojo, pop. 35,000), 450km (279 miles). Situated on the shore of Lake Lohjajärvi, this is one of the most recent business and service centres to have sprung up around Helsinki. It's possible to descend 110m (360ft) below ground in the town's **Tytyri Mine Museum** (June to August daily 11am–6pm, May and September to December noon–4pm).

Those with more time on their hands should consider taking one of the more minor roads to the south, running parallel to the route described above, and passing through the rural municipalities of Karjaa, Pohja, Perniö and Kemiö. Fine views of the sea here alternate with forests of oak, and the many small factories dotted along the route bear witness to the fact that this area was the cradle of Finnish industrialisation.

Signs of early industry

Route 4

The West Coast *See map, pages 32–3*

Helsinki – Espoo – Ekenäs – Hanko – Salo – Turku – Naantali – Uusikaupunki – Rauma – Pori – Kristiinankaupunki – Vaasa – Laihia – Kurikka – Parkano – Huittinen – Turku (901km/559 miles). *Note: mileage given beside a town name represents how far along the route it is.*

This route takes us along the edge of the Gulf of Bothnia. The area is the home of the Finland-Swedes, who are bilingual and quite different from other Finns. The towns here largely escaped wartime destruction, and several of them contain fascinating old buildings; the long, sandy beaches are also a big attraction. All the Finnish towns along the west coast have Swedish names, too (often used interchangeably by the local inhabitants); these are given in brackets after their Finnish names.

The beaches are a big attraction

The route outlined here takes around three to four days, and leads from Helsinki to Turku (181km/112 miles) before describing a large arc (720km/447 miles).

39

It is difficult to recognise the suburban area of **Espoo** (Espo, pop. 217,000, www.espootravel.com) as a city because it is so spread out. One of the first areas of Finland to be settled, it was given its **Tapiola Garden City** in 1951. Built as a self-contained town rather than a dormitory suburb, Tapiola is populated by people from all walks of life. Any visit to Espoo should also include the **Otaniemi University** campus and the **Dipoli Congress Centre**, a strikingly successful Finnish amphitheatre. It was here that the famous Helsinki Accords were signed in 1975, which recognised the inviolability of the post-World War II frontiers in Europe, and pledged the 35 signatory nations to protect human rights and other fundamental freedoms.

The Tapiola Centre

The representatives of the various nations who met for the first time in 1972 at the Dipoli Congress Centre were initially interested only in strengthening their respective positions: America wanted to use the conference as a propaganda weapon against the USSR, and the latter thought it would further cement the division of Germany. The Accords were finally signed on 1 August 1975. The fourth Conference on Security and Cooperation in Europe (CSCE) was held in Helsinki again in 1992 in a Europe that had changed beyond recognition: Germany was reunified, the USSR had dissolved and the Baltic countries had regained sovereignty. Finland's neutral role was no longer important, and the 'spirit of the Accords' had at last triumphed.

Outside Espoo the former home and workshop of the painter and designer Akseli Gallen-Kallela has been turned into the **Gallen-Kallela Museum** (Tarvaspää Gallen-Kallelantie 27, summer daily 10am–6pm).

It was in Tapiola and Otaniemi that Eliel Saarinen, Armas Lindgren and Hermann Geselius turned many of their architectural dreams into reality. Their National Romantic visions are reflected in the fortress-like granite-and-pine villa of ★★ **Hvitträsk** (summer daily 10am–6pm; winter 11am–6pm), built in 1902 in **Kirkkonummi**, 30km (18 miles) away from Helsinki (take exit III off the E3). With this studio and residential complex the three architects created a 'Finlandia of architecture', described by Eliel Saarinen as his 'Finnish dream'. The architecture and interior design combines elements from Karelian farmhouses, medieval castles and art nouveau to form a harmonious, if somewhat wilful, composition. Today the villa is a living museum and also a holiday centre, with a restaurant and overnight accommodation.

The road leading to the idyllic town of **Ekenäs** (Tammisaari, pop. 14,600, www.ekenas.fi), 70km (43 miles), is full of ups and downs. Ekenäs is the second-oldest town in Uusimaa province, and received its royal charter from King Gustav Vasa in 1546. The town is still predominantly Swedish-speaking, and a stroll through its old section, the **Barcken Peninsula** with its old church, is like walking back into the past. The beaches are great, and the **Ramsholmen Nature Park**, situated out on a headland, has many rare plants and songbirds. Another good excursion from here is to the ruined 13th-century castle of **Raasepori**, named after the German town of Ratzeburg by merchants from Lübeck.

Visitors to Raasepori
The marina at Hanko

Just 37km (22 miles) away from Ekenäs, at the southwestern corner of Finland, is **Hanko** (Hangö, pop. 10,000,

www.hanko.fi). Its protected natural harbour has been valued for centuries, and the strategically important peninsula was leased out to the Soviet Union as a naval base between 1940 and 1941. Today Hanko, with its 30 beaches, casino and annual regatta is a mecca for holidaymakers and mariners. The best view of the town is from the 50m (164ft) high Vartiovuori Water Tower, which also contains a lift.

The **Rocks of Gäddtarmen** near the narrow sound of **Hauensuoli** (waterbus links twice daily from east harbour) bear the coats-of-arms and names of many merchants, warriors and nobles who travelled past them from the 15th century to the present. Carry on via Salo now towards Turku. A good detour just 20km (12 miles) short of Turku is ★ **Parainen** (Pargas) with its suspension bridge across the **Kirjalansalmi Sound**, affording superb views across the water. Small 17th-century houses line the narrow streets of the Parainen suburb of Malmi. The church here, which dates from 1320, is as grey as the local quarry.

Parainen suspension bridge

A side-road 14km (8 miles) west of Turku *(see page 28)* leads to **Naantali** (Nadendal, pop. 13,300). This dignified little town comes alive every summer when the Finnish president comes to stay at his summer retreat of **Kultaranta** here (visits through prior arrangement with tourist office); less important people move into their summer houses in the old town centre, with its narrow winding streets. In Naantali people go out for strolls in order to be noticed, and tend to retreat to their yachts in the evenings. The real hit for children here is ★ **Moomin World** (12 June to 15 August 10am–6pm), based on the characters made famous by Finnish author Tove Jansson.

41

Moomin World is a hit

Continue further northwards now; there's an optional short detour via **Askainen** (Askais), where Marshal Mannerheim was born. The harbour town of **Uusikaupunki** (Nystad, pop. 17,000), 70km (43 miles), was founded in 1617 by Gustav II. Today its only real claim to fame is its car factory – the only one in Finland. The municipal park also contains several picturesque windmills – and those eager to visit an unusual museum should definitely stop by the rather oddly-named **Dynamokeskus Bonk** (summer daily 10am–6pm; other times Monday to Friday, 10am–4pm) at Siltakatu 2. This little museum has a collection of machines with one feature in common: none of them actually works. Should any of them happen to start functioning, one thing is certain – they have absolutely no productive use whatsoever.

Another seaside town is ★ **Rauma** (Raumo, pop. 37,000), 118km (73 miles). The third-oldest town in Finland, it received its charter in 1442, and is based on a medieval ground-plan. It also contains Scandinavia's

Rauma

Wooden house interior

Making lace

largest intact ★★★ **wooden house quarter**. The **Kiikar Tower** provides a good view of the whole town. Rauma is also a traditional lacemaking centre, and there's a special lace week at the end of June every year. The **Old Town Hall** dates from 1776, and contains a small lace, seafaring and shipbuilding museum (summer daily 10am–5pm, otherwise Tuesday to Friday and Sunday 10am–5pm, Saturday 10am–2pm, Sunday lacemaking demonstrations 2–5pm). Another worthwhile sight in Rauma is the **Pyhän Ristin kirkko**, a 15th-century Franciscan monastery church; anyone feeling hungry should certainly sample the town's culinary speciality, peppered pancakes.

The town of **Pori** (Björneborg, pop. 76,000), 167km (103 miles), at the mouth of the Kokemäenjoki river, was founded in 1558. The fact that this part of Finland is gradually rising out of the sea has already placed the centre of Pori 20km (12 miles) away from the actual coast, where summer beach life takes place in the dunes of ★ **Yyteri**. Pori itself is not only a centre of industry but also of culture: the first ever theatre in Finland was founded here, the Pori Jazz Festival on Kirjurinluoto Island is the musical high point of the year, and the Venetian-inspired **Town Hall** (Hallituskatu 12) is of architectural interest. A good local excursion is the fishing village of **Reposaari**, 32km (19 miles) away.

The dunes near Yyteri

Founded by Peter Brahe in 1649, the little town of **Kristiinankaupunki** (Kristinestad, pop. 8,000), 264km (164 miles), has been spared the ravages of fire and flood over the years. The colourful wooden houses have stood here since the 18th century, and romantic streets such as ★ **Kissanpiiskaajankuja** and **Miilukuja** are great places to stroll. Don't miss the old **Tullituvat** customs house. The **Lappfjärd Church** was built in 1852 and can hold 3,000 people, while the **Ulrike Eleonora Church** (1700) is the oldest wooden church in southern Ostrobothnia.

Ulrike Eleonora Church

The last stop along the coast is **Vaasa** (Vasa, pop. 57,000, www.vaasa.fi), 364km (226 miles). Its geographical location at the narrowest point of the Gulf of Bothnia has meant that its fortunes were always closely connected with those of Sweden (beware of crowds of drunken Swedes who come here by ferry to escape their own country's severe alcohol laws). The municipality of ★ **Mustasaari** (which has an excellent music festival every June) has enjoyed trading privileges since the 13th century. Old Vaasa, founded in 1606, was completely destroyed by a fire on 3 August 1852, when a farmer fell asleep with his pipe in his mouth while visiting a merchant. The new Vaasa was built in Empire style on the Klemetsö Peninsula according to designs by the architect CA Setterberg. The town has a cosmopolitan atmosphere, not least because of the ferry connections from here to Umeå and Sundsvall in Sweden. A good way to follow up a stroll through the centre of Old Vaasa is to visit the **Brage Open-Air Museum** (summer Tuesday to Friday 1–6pm, Saturday and Sunday noon–4pm, Monday closed) in the suburb of Hietalahti with its fascinating collection of various farmhouses. Children will love the **Vasalandia Amusement Park** on the Vaskiluoto peninsula.

Vassa has a cosmopolitan feel

43

The journey back across flat, fertile fields goes via **Laihia**, which happily markets its reputation as the stingiest town in Finland by peddling such things as ladles with holes in the bottom, etc. A little further south the landscape suddenly starts getting hilly and in **Kurikka**, 439km (272 miles), there's a fine stone church designed by CL Engel which was built in 1847. Now the route passes through a series of young, ambitious industrial communities along the western edge of the Helsinki–Turku–Tampere triangle. Among them is **Parkano**, which only received its civic charter in 1977. Not far away is the impressive scenery of the **Seitseminen Nature Conservation Park**.

In **Hämeenkyrö**, visit the **birthplace of FE Sillanpää** (1 June to 16 August noon–6pm), the only Finnish novelist to win the Nobel Prize for Literature, in 1939. Not far from the museum, the **Kyröskoski Rapids** are a spectacular sight; the waterfall is 21m (68ft) high. From here the route continues on to **Vammala** and the austere beauty of its **Pirunvuori** (Devil's Mountain) on the large island of **Salonsaari**, and then further to **Huittinen**, 630km (391 miles). Huittinen marks the confluence of the Kokemäenjoki, the Loimijoki and the Punkalaitumenjoki; the nearby **Puurijärvi-Isosuo National Park** is a famous bird sanctuary. The route finally ends up in Turku *(see page 28).*

Route 5

A Musical Trail *See map, pages 32–3*

Tampere – Orivesi – Keuruu – Kaustinen – Kokkola – Pietarsaari – Uusikaarlepyy – Lapua – Seinäjoki – Virrat – Ruovesi – Tampere (700km/434 miles).
Note: mileage given beside a town name represents how far along the route it is.

This whole trip can be done in three to four days; in July, when the musicians start their weekend performances in Kaustinen or Seinäjoki, the time just flies by. The round trip starts in Tampere. Crossing the western part of the lake region and then heading through central Ostrobothnia, it features all the different faces of the Finnish landscape: bays, lakes, bare rock, deep gorges and thick forest. The scenic beauty of this region is enhanced by the various entertainment possibilities for old and young alike. It's a good idea to combine this car journey with a boat excursion.

A cross-section of Finnish nature can be experienced in **Orivesi** (pop. 9,000), just 45km (27 miles) away from Tampere. Its many quarries provide an essential component of Finnish culture – the special stones used in sauna ovens. The ★ **Eräjärvi Stone Museum** (1 June to 31 August Tuesday to Sunday noon–6pm, otherwise by prior arrangement, tel: 03-530 6416) has a collection of 400 different types of stone including some rare minerals.

The journey continues through forest, past several signs warning motorists about the fondness that Finnish elk have for crossing the road just at the wrong moment. It's easy to lose your bearings in this landscape with all its lakes and bays. One very pleasant way to travel through this maze is to take an old paddle steamer: the *Elias Lönnrot* does small daily cruises in the summer from **Keuruu** (pop. 11,700), 120km (74 miles). The impression of everything being the same – meadows and farmland intermingling with forests – becomes hypnotic as the journey continues.

The next major population centre appears 80km (49 miles) further on: **Karstula**, an excellent base for canoeing trips along the nearby rivers. The town of **Kaustinen** (pop. 4,500), 305km (189 miles), situated at the gateway to the Gulf of Bothnia, was one of the first communities in this region to have a music festival. Now known familiarly as 'the village of folk music', this tiny provincial town has become a mecca for folk music enthusiasts. The music is mostly authentic, and attracts over 3,000 musicians and dancers from all over the world every summer. The festival is held during the third week of July, but folk music

The Stone Museum

Elias Lönnrot and the surrounding landscape

is alive and well here at other times of the year too, as is clear from a visit to the ★ **Village Musician House** (Monday to Friday 10am–2pm, also Sunday in summer).

Soon the coastal towns make their appearance. **Kokkola** (pop. 36,000), 350km (217 miles), is the economic centre of Ostrobothnia, and was founded in the year 1620 by the Swedish king Gustav II. The architect Carl Ludwig Engel also made his mark here: his **Town Hall** was built in 1842. Kokkola also has three very good museums: the **Art Museum**, the **Historical Museum** and the **Renlund Museum** (15 May to 31 August Tuesday to Sunday noon–6pm). The last contains the painting collection bequeathed to the town by Renlund, a wealthy merchant. Kokkola's ★★ **wooden house quarter** is also definitely worth a visit, and the town as a whole still has a real seafaring feel to it.

Continue further via the so-called **Seven Bridge Route**, a stretch of great scenic beauty which crosses the islands of Larsmo. Note the life-sized wooden statues outside the churches, begging churchgoers for alms. The oldest of these in Ostrobothnia is the one outside the church in **Larsmo** (Luoto); it was carved in 1782. The town of **Pietarsaari** (Jakobstad, pop. 19,500), 390km (242 miles), has even more of a maritime feel to it than Kokkola. The **Wanha Satama** amusement complex is definitely worth a visit, and an architecturally interesting collection of buildings recently appeared next to it on the occasion of the 1994 national home exhibition. That same year the *Jakobstad Wapen*, a reconstruction of an 18th-century ship, first set sail. Other sights in Pietarsaari include the richly decorated **Town Hall** with its coat-of-arms on the tower, and also the ★ **municipal church**, which dates back to medieval times – though ever since it was extended to form a classical domed church with a cloister in 1787 its exterior has been more reminiscent of a Mexican *hacienda*. The Finnish national poet JL Runeberg was born here in Pietarsaari in 1804, and there are several guided tours following in his footsteps. On sunny summer days, a good place to head for is the **Fäboda Recreation Area**, with its seemingly endless sandy beaches and rocky cliffs.

Pietarsaari has a maritime feel

Further south along the 749 road is the typically Finnish small town of **Uusikaarlepyy** (Nykarleby, pop. 7,500), 410km (254 miles), with its parks, statues and old wooden houses. The town was founded in 1620, and is dominated by the ★ **Church of St Bridget**, built in 1708 (summer 9am–6pm); the copper weathervane on top of the tower was acquired at great expense in Stockholm in 1709. Before taking the 67 road inland at this point, it's worth paying a quick visit to ★ **Kudnäs Mansion** (May, Tuesday

Kudnäs Mansion

Lapua Cathedral

Traditional village

The Runeberg Springs

to Sunday 10am–3pm, June to July Tuesday to Sunday 10am–5pm, August Tuesday to Sunday noon–5pm) where the poet, painter and journalist Sakari Topelius was born in 1818. In addition to writing an extraordinarily large number of books, he also did a great deal to further the interests of the working classes.

The architect CL Engel also had a hand in the design of an important building in **Lapua** (Lappo, pop. 14,000), 485km (301 miles). The ★ **cathedral** was built according to plans drawn up by Engel and Kuorikoski, and it contains the largest organ in Finland (6,660 pipes).

The town of **Seinäjoki** (pop. 30,700) not only boasts the ★ **South Ostrobothnian Agricultural Museum** with its farmhouses and tools, but also a **gunpowder museum**, a **watermill museum** and a **pharmaceutical museum**. The biggest draw here, however, is the **Tango Fair**, which is held in the first week of July every year. It was started in 1985, and the music has its own, characteristically Finnish edge: the minor keys are definitely preferred. Nearly 100,000 visitors make the pilgrimage here each year. By way of contrast, lovers of classical music will definitely enjoy the festival at nearby **Ilmajoki**.

Another short detour is strongly recommended at this point for families with young children: the **Ähtäri Wildlife Park** contains domestic Finnish animals in their natural forest habitat; its **domestic pet park** contains all the animals one expects to find on an average Finnish farm; and its **Mini-Finland Theme Park** provides visitors with a great deal of information on the country as a whole.

Virrat (Virdois, www.virrat.fi), 590km (366 miles), the northernmost municipality in Häme province, contains the **Herraskoski Canal** (constructed between 1903 and 1907) and also a fascinating ★ **traditional village** (4km/2½ miles from the centre in the direction of Pori). The surrounding wild landscape with its high rocks, dark forests and deep lakes makes this region an ideal base for hiking and canoeing trips. Take a trip on the *Tarjanne*, a romantic steamer. It travels along the Virrat–Ruovesi–Tampere route (Wednesday, Friday, Sunday; opposite direction Tuesday, Thursday, Saturday), also known as the *Poet's Way* in memory of JL Runeberg, who often praised the scenic beauty of this part of the country. The village of **Ruovesi**, 630km (391 miles), has a fascinating folk museum with 23 buildings typical of the region. Afterwards the **Runeberg Springs** provide a refreshing drop of mineral water.

On the journey back the route passes the **Helvetinjärvi** (Devil's Lake) with the deep ravine next to it known as **Helvetinkolu**. This is where guided wilderness tours end over a meal of fire-smoked rainbow trout.

Route 6

Exploring the Heart of Finland's Lake Region *See map, pages 32–3*

Jyväskylä (boat trip Lahti–Hollola–Heinola–Lahti) – Saarijärvi –Viitasaari – Pihtipudas – Pyhäsalmi – Iisalmi – Kuopio (490km/304 miles). *Note: mileage given beside a town name represents how far along the route it is.*

Land of a Thousand Lakes

Before travelling through the region that has earned Finland the name 'Land of a Thousand Lakes', it's worth mentioning the very Finnish concept of a *mökki*. The word is best translated as 'summer-house by the water', and the Finns adore them. A *mökki* can be anything from a ramshackle wooden hut to a full-blown luxury cabin, and Finland is full of them. Keep an eye out for *mökki* along this route; they're usually located in idyllic surroundings.

Finland is full of mökkis

This route takes a good three days to cover by car. We begin it, though, with a two-day-long boat trip to Lahti.

The starting-point and final destination of the boat-trip part of this route is **Jyväskylä** (pop. 80,000 www.jyvaskyla.fi), the largest town in central Finland, situated on the northern shore of Lake Päijänne. The town's biggest claim to fame is the fact that the legendary Finnish architect Alvar Aalto (1898–1976) grew up here, and it has more than its fair share of buildings designed by him: the police station, the university, the civic theatre and the Museum of Central Finland. Don't miss a visit to the ★ **Alvar Aalto Museum** (Alvar Aallon Katu 7, Tuesday to Sunday 11am–6pm) either, which has a collection of plans, photos and scale models. The best exhibits, however, are out on the streets. There's

Alvar Aalto's theatre

Service at Savutuvan Apaja

One stretch of water after another

The lakes are great for swimming

also ★ **Savutuvan Apaja** (5 June to 7 August Sunday to Friday 11am–6pm), an open-air museum just outside the town in Vaajakoski which has earned much critical acclaim.

The only way to become really immersed in the solemn beauty of the Finnish lake region is to take a boat trip out across it (preferably in the company of Sibelius), and the following is a recommended two-day journey from Jyväskylä to Lahti and then back again. The trip across Lake Päijänne, the second-largest lake in Finland, takes ten hours, and roughly at the halfway mark the boat passes the attractive bridges of Pulkkilanharju, which span the sounds of Karisälmi, Pulkkilanharju and Käkisalmi. At the scenically very beautiful Asikkalanselkä the trip then continues via the 1,306m (4,284ft) long Vääksy Canal, which was completed in 1871, and connects Lake Päijänne with Lake Vesijärvi; it runs parallel to the bed of a river which once connected the two stretches of water.

The town of **Lahti** (Lahtis, pop. 97,000, www.lahtitravel.fi) had a population of only 200 at the beginning of the 20th century. It owes its present-day fame to the **Salpausselkä** range of hills where several important Nordic skiing competitions are now regularly held. The five enormous ski-jumps hang over the town, with a swimming-pool beneath them (in winter it's frozen over and is used as a landing area); a lift takes visitors up to the observation platform on the highest ski-jump, where there's a breathtaking view of the town below and the surrounding forests and lakes. Lahti's sudden rise to prominence began at the end of World War II. Its population doubled within 20 years because of the steady influx of Karelians, most of whom moved here from Vyborg after it was claimed by the Soviet Union.

There are several good examples of 20th-century Finnish architecture in the town including Eliel Saarinen's red-brick Town Hall (1912), and Alvar Aalto's Church of the Cross (Ristin kirkko, 1978), the last church he designed. Lahti also has an interesting **Skiing Museum** (Monday to Friday 10am–5pm, Saturday and Sunday 11am–5pm); and Pyhäniemi Manor in **Hollola**, a few miles northwest of the town, is also definitely worth a visit. Should you happen to arrive in Lahti by car, a good substitute boat trip is the one-day steamer connection from Lahti to Heinola and back.

The town of **Heinola** (pop. 21,000) lies on the banks of the Jyrängönvirta. Lakes, hills and the 924m (3,031ft) long **Heinolan Tähti suspension bridge** are among the most striking features here. Other highlights include the wooden church, which was built in 1811, with its free-standing campanile, and also the bird sanctuary (Lintutarha) to which admission is free.

The second day is taken up with the return journey from Lahti across Lake Päijänne. Back in Jyväskylä, the car trip can now begin. The first stage on the route is to the 360-year-old town of ★ **Saarijärvi** (pop. 10,300), 46km (28 miles), situated on a promontory and surrounded by three lakes. The **Stone Age Village** documents the earliest settlement here, and the **Museum of Aquatic Life** in Kolkkalahti has exhibits illustrating the various types of fauna to be found in, on and beside the water; there's also a fishing village and amusement park nearby.

There are very few roads in this part of the lake region, but that's more than compensated for by the superb scenery near **Viitasaari** (pop. 7,800), 108km (67 miles) at the top of Lake Keitele: thundering rapids and incredibly steep rockfaces combine to create a lasting impression of wild beauty. Good hikers should try out the ascent of **Karoliina's Steps** next to Lake Kymönkoski (9km/5 miles from Viitasaari in the direction of Pihtipudas); the view from the top more than rewards the strenuous climb.

Viitasaari rapids and along Karoliina's steps

Continue northwestwards now via **Pihtipudas**, 146km (90 miles), where a javelin throwing festival is held every July. At Pyhäsalmi, 190km (118 miles), there's an optional turn-off from the E4 along the 87 road in the direction of Haapamäki, a superb place to go salmon fishing.

The town of **Iisalmi** (pop. 23,000, www.iisalmenseutu.info), 258km (160 miles) takes its name from the Same word meaning 'night' – possibly because quite a few travellers spend the night on the shore of the bay here. It's rather unusual to be greeted at a hotel reception by an Orthodox priest, but that's what happens at the ★★ **Evakkokeskus** (Kyllikinkatu 8, daily 9am–6pm) because it's a cross between an Orthodox centre and a hotel, and Father Elias is the manager. The frescoes in the refectory were done by

Refectory frescoes at Evakkokeskus

a Greek painter named Dimitros Andonopoulos. Iisalmi also has what is probably the smallest restaurant in the world: the ★ **Korkki** was built in 1907 as a waiting room for railway passengers, and has enough room for just three people – two diners and a staff of one. In addition to the 'dining-hall' section there's a terrace with two more chairs. That's not all Iisalmi has to offer, though – it's also the home of the legendary and delicious *Olmi* beer. Academic interest in the subject is catered for by the **Brewery Museum** at the harbour, and for the thirsty the best time to arrive here is during the Oluset Beer Festival in July.

Kuopio market building and market goers

This route now continues on to **Kuopio** (pop. 87,000, www.kuopioinfo.fi), 349km (216 miles), in the province of Savo, home of a very different breed of Finn with a mentality often envied by the rest of the country. Even those not versed in either Finnish or Savo dialect will quickly notice that Kuopio's market women proudly sell a local speciality, *kalakukko* (a chunk of bread with pork and whitefish baked inside it) – and some people reckon it can only be really properly enjoyed when accompanied by Kuopio's second speciality, *mesimarja*, a liqueur made from Arctic raspberries. The ★ **market square** at the centre of the town (May to September Monday to Friday 7am–5pm, Saturday 7am–3pm; otherwise Monday to Friday 7am–3pm, Saturday 7am–2pm) isn't the only lively place by any means – there's the open-air stage outside the Town Hall, for instance, where all kinds of music from rock to classical can be enjoyed. Kuopio can also be admired from above, by the way: the observation tower on the **Puijo Hill** with its revolving restaurant provides a fantastic view of the town with all the lakes around it.

Kuopio was founded in 1782 by King Gustav III of Sweden, but only really began to prosper after the opening of the Saimaa Waterway in 1856. The famous Finnish nationalist **J V Snellman** lived and worked here during the mid-19th century, and his former **home** (May to September daily 10am–5pm, Wednesday until 7pm; October to April by appointment) at Snellmaninkatu 19 is open to the public. The real highlight of Kuopio, however, is the ★ **Orthodox Church Museum** (Karjalankatu 1, 2 May to 31 August Tuesday to Sunday 10am–4pm), which has a magnificent collection of Orthodox church treasures, saved from the Soviet occupied Valamo monastery on Lake Ladoga.

Orthodox Museum treasure

The medical faculty at Kuopio University has earned itself an international reputation for its research into heart surgery, but perhaps of more interest to visitors is the annual festival of music and dance in June. It features all kinds of international names, from the Bolshoi Ballet to the Chinese Opera.

Route 7

The Saimaa *See map, pages 32–3*

Porvoo – Loviisa – Kotka – (optional detour to Hamina) – Kouvola – Lappeenranta – Imatra – Punkaharju – Savonlinna – Varkaus – Mikkeli – Lappeenranta (970km/602 miles). *Note: mileage given beside a town name represents how far along the route it is.*

This round trip follows a figure-of-eight route through the eastern part of Europe's fourth-largest lake region, the Saimaa, and the initial section leading to it passes through several historically important towns between Helsinki and the Russian border. The whole route is 970km (602 miles) long, and can be covered by car in three to four days.

The river at Porvoo

The town of **Porvoo** (Borga, pop. 45,000. www.porvoo.fi), 50km (31 miles), has had a civic charter since 1346 and is one of the oldest towns along the south coast. The red ★ **granary buildings** along the banks of the Provonjoki convey some of the former atmosphere of this once-important trading centre. The fortress of **Linnamäki** (Borgbacken) was erected around 1200 to protect the town, and there's a good panoramic view from the small rise on which it stands. From the old bridge there's also a good view across to the old ★ **cathedral**, which dates from 1418 and towers above the picturesque ★ **Old Town**. In this cathedral, in 1809, the Finnish nation was born, when Tsar Alexander I proclaimed the country a Russian grand duchy, himself grand duke, and convened the first Finnish Diet. Many Finnish artists have lived in Porvoo over the years, and the **Runeberg House** (Aleksanterinkatu 3, summer 10am–4pm, Sunday 11am–5pm, winter Wednesday to Sunday) stands in memory of one of them, the national poet JL Runeberg, who spent 25 years of his life here.

51

Runeberg's home

The next stop on this route is **Loviisa** (Lovisa, pop. 7,500), 89km (55 miles), founded as a trading centre in 1745. The border between (Swedish) Finland and Russia used to be located near here between 1743 and 1809, before it was shifted east of the Kymijoki. The centre of Loviisa was rebuilt in 1805 – the town was once a famous spa resort – and is a superb place for a stroll. There are generally far fewer tourists here than in nearby Porvoo. Today Loviisa's name is most often connected with Finland's first **nuclear power station** (Hästholmen Island, guided tours in summer, Sunday 12.30pm, bus from main bus station). The growing anti-nuclear movement in Finland is now calling for a switch to hydroelectric power, and the view of the power station in the bay is rather unnerving when

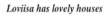

Loviisa has lovely houses

Tsar's fishing lodge, Langinkoski

Industry in Kotka

you consider the design flaws of Soviet-built reactors. Loviisanlahti Bay is a popular excursion destination during the summer, however, because it also contains the impressive remains of the maritime fortress of ★ **Svatholma**, which was destroyed in 1855 during the Crimean War. The journey continues from here to Kotka, passing the excellent sandy beaches of Pyhtää on the way, and also the holiday island of Kaunissaari with its interesting fishing village – both good places to stop.

The town of **Kotka** (pop. 54,800, www.kotka.fi/matkailu), 134km (83 miles), is enormous compared to most of the other little communities between here and Helsinki, and its combination of beach and industry, river scenery and agriculture, harbour and history is most compelling. A stroll through ★ **Langinkoski**, the town's park, is very relaxing; it contains some fine rapids and also the **Imperial Fishing Lodge** (1889), where Tsar Alexander II used to rest while in transit between Helsinki and St Petersburg. Bombardment in 1855 by a British fleet during the Crimean War destroyed much of the town along with its Russian-built fortifications, but the Orthodox **church of St Nicholas** (1795) was miraculously spared. A memorial on **Varisaari Island** (motor-boat connections) commemorates Europe's greatest sea battle, in which 500 ships took part; it was fought off the coast here in 1790. Why not take a trip on the world's oldest steam-driven icebreaker, the ★ *Tarmo*? It was built in England in 1907 and is moored in the harbour at Kantasatama. A good time to come to Kotka is at the beginning of August when the **Sea Shanty Festival** is held in the harbour, which is the largest in Finland.

The town of **Hamina** (Fredrikshamn, pop. 9,800) is a good detour at this point; to get there follow the old 'royal' route in the direction of Vyborg and St Petersburg. The big attraction here is the ★ **concentric town plan** centred around an octagonal market-place from which eight streets radiate outwards. At the centre of the town is the **Town Hall** (1789, rebuilt in 1840 by CL Engel). Hamina was originally called Vekhalahti when it was founded in the 14th century, and it only received its civic charter in 1653. When it suddenly found itself close to the Russian border after the Peace of Uusikaupunki in 1721, the Swedes built fortifications here to compensate for Vyborg, which had fallen to the Russians. The fortification work was still incomplete when the Russians marched into the town in 1742, and the latter continued fortifying the place until 1812 without a shot being fired. The military tradition is still alive and well here: Hamina is an important training centre for the Finnish army and also hosts the country's annual festival of military music. The town's colourful market-place is a far less organised affair altogether, and definitely deserves a visit.

Part of a long military tradition

Back on the main route, the next stop is ★ **Anjalankoski**. The rapids in the Kymijoki here are favourites with canoeists and river-rafters, but another popular sight is **Anjala Manor** (15 May to 15 August 11am–5pm), built at the end of the 18th century, and now a museum.

53

The town of **Kouvola** (pop. 32,000), 188km (116 miles), the capital of the province of Kymi, is the last stop before the tour of the Saimaa. It has a good amusement park (summer daily noon–8pm, otherwise Saturday noon–9pm), and there's also a fine miniature **zoo** in the suburb of Tykkimäki (open all year round), a good place to take young children.

The Saimaa Lake Region has 50,000km (30,000 miles) of shoreline – a distance longer than the circumference of the earth. This tour begins in **Lappeenranta** (Villmanstrand, pop. 58,400, www.lappeenranta.fi), 280km (173 miles), a town at the northern end of the Saimaa Waterway. It was granted its civic charter in 1649 by the Swedish queen Kristina. Totally destroyed in 1741, the town only experienced an economic upswing after it was reincorporated into Sweden in 1811. The 50km (31 mile) long ★ **Saimaa Waterway** begins in the industrial suburb of Lauritsala and connects the lake region with the Gulf of Finland. Originally completed in 1856, it was renovated in 1968 and since 1991 has also been used by excursion traffic headed for Vyborg in Russia. The **fortress** next to the harbour in Lappeenranta was erected by the Russians in 1775. The town has several interesting churches, including Finland's oldest Orthodox church (1785) in the suburb of Linnoitus near the fortress, and the temple-like 'Light of Heaven' church in the suburb of Lauritsala. Perhaps the most interesting place

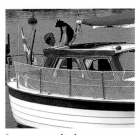
Lappeenranta harbour

Finland's oldest Orthodox church

Olavinlinna Castle

Imatrankoski rapids

to visit here in Lappeenranta, however, is the **Museum of Southern Karelia** (Kristiinankatu, June to mid-August Monday to Friday 10am–6pm, Saturday and Sunday 11am–5pm; mid-August to May Tuesday to Sunday 11am–5pm) with its fascinating collection of exhibits documenting the history of the Finnish town of **Viipuri**, 60km (37 miles) away from Lappeenranta, which was ceded to the Russians in 1940 and again in 1944. Once an important town on the Saimaa Waterway, Viipuri was simply left to decay by the Soviet Union; many of its former inhabitants still live here in Lappeenranta.

The route continues now through some dense areas of forest along the border to the town of **Imatra** (pop. 30,400, www.travel.imatra.fi), 314km (195 miles), founded on the banks of the Vuoksi river in 1948. The town owes its swift transformation into a centre of heavy industry to the nearby power station on the ★★ **Imatrankoski Rapids**. The huge mass of excess water that is discharged from the power station every summer (weekdays 7pm, Sunday, 3pm) is an impressive sight. The whole scene is framed by the **Kruununpuisto Park** with its oak trees and observation pavilion. Day trips to the Russian towns of Svetogorsk and Kamennogorsk can also be organised from here.

The journey continues along what is probably one of the best-known scenic landmarks in all of Finland, the 7km (4 mile) long ★★ **Punkaharju Ridge**. Narrow and elegant, this strip of land divides lakes Pihlajavesi and Puruvesi, and the old road along it *(vanha tie)* is never more than a few metres away from the water's edge. The ridge passes by the amazing ★★ **Retretti Arts Centre**, made up of a series of caves gouged out of the ancient rock and also a sculpture park, containing all manner of strange artworks.

The route now reaches the relaxed tourist resort of **Savonlinna** (pop. 27,700, www.travel.fi/ssavonlinna), 433km (269 miles), which is spread across a series of interconnected islands. The real highlight here is ★★★ **Olavinlinna**, the best-preserved medieval castle in the whole of Finland (guided tours daily 2 January to 31 May 10am–3pm, 1 June to 15 August 10am–5pm, 16 August to 23 December 10am–3pm). It was founded in 1475 to guard the disputed border between Sweden and Russia, and the walls on the eastern side of the castle are 5m (16ft) thick. The castle changed hands quite often over the years, however. Savonlinna's other claim to fame is its internationally renowned ★★ **Opera Festival**, lasting the whole of July *(see page 79)*, for which tickets usually need to be bought well in advance.

A night at the opera

There's music of a different kind to be experienced in nearby **Varkaus** (pop. 23,200, www.varkaus.fi), 520km (323 miles), in the **Mechanical Music Museum** (Pelimannikatu 8, 15 March to 11 December Tuesday to Sunday 11am–7pm, July daily 10am–8pm); here all kinds of ancient devices including a pianola can be admired. Varkaus is built across several canals, and the Taipale Canal, dating from 1839, is the oldest in Finland. One very worthwhile excursion is to the Orthodox monastery of **Valamo**, in the Heinävesi district halfway between Varkaus and Joensuu. The original monastery lay on Lake Ladoga and was the spiritual headquarters of Orthodox Karelia from the 12th century, but when the Russians were on the point of invading in 1939, it was shifted well inside the Finnish border.

55

After rounding Lake Haukivesi and Lake Orivesi (via Joensuu, 641km/398 miles, *see Route 8, page 56*), there's another fascinating sight just 23km (14 miles) outside Savonlinna in the village of **Kerimäki**, 761km (472 miles). The huge **wooden church** here was built in 1848; it can hold 5,000 people, and is said to be the largest wooden church in the world (June to August Monday to Friday 9am–8pm, Saturday 9am–6pm, Sunday 11am–8pm).

World's largest wooden church

The figure-of-eight route now intersects in the middle at **Mikkeli** (St Michel, pop. 46,600, www.travel.fi/mikkeli), 861km (535 miles), situated between Lake Saimaa and Lake Puulajärvi. The **Kenkävero** handicraft centre (Pursialankatu 6, Sunday to Friday 10am–6pm, Saturday 10am–4pm, July 10am–7pm) is housed inside the oldest vicarage in Finland; there is also a wax museum at the **Visulahti** recreation centre. Mikkeli has a military past: it was from here that General Mannerheim conducted his campaign against the Soviet Union in the Winter War, and the room in which he actually won the war is now the **Headquarters Museum** (Päämanjankatu 1–3, May to August daily 11am–5pm).

Crafts at the Kenkävero

This tour of the eastern part of the Saimaa lake system now ends back in Lappeenranta (970km/602 miles).

Rural transport in Karelia

Route 8

Finnish Karelia *See map, pages 32–3*

Joensuu – Tohmajärvi – Kypärävaara – Värtsilä – Mutalahti –Iilomantsi – Lieksa – Vuonisjärvi – Ruunaa Rapids – Nurmes – Ukko-Koli – Joensuu (480km/298 miles). *Note: mileage given beside a town name represents how far along the route it is.*

The Karelians live on either side of the Finno-Russian border. Many Finns consider the inhabitants of the province of Northern Karelia to be among the friendliest and most open, spontaneous people in Finland. This one- to two-day-long car tour explores the part of the country where Elias Lönnrot collected much of the material for his *Kalevala* folk epic. Nature in Finnish Karelia is still intact, and bear, lynx and wolverine are very much at home here.

This round trip begins in **Joensuu** (pop. 52,000, www.jns.fi), capital of the province of Northern Karelia. The border with Russia can be crossed by Finns (and anyone else) with a valid Russian visa. The Pielisjoki river, rendered navigable along a length of 65km (40 miles) by 11 sluices, is one of the most important lumber transport routes in Finland. The **Museum of Northern Karelia** (Carelicum, Koskikatu 5, Monday to Friday 10am–5pm, Saturday and Sunday 11am–5pm) gives a good impression of the history and the traditions of the region. In mid-June up to 11,000 singers take part in the **Joensuu Song Festival** in the enormous **Song Bowl** southwest of the town centre.

The trip continues southwards now across an unusually beautiful stretch of hilly landscape to **Tohmajärvi** (pop. 5,200), 68km (42 miles), the birthplace of Maiju Lassila. This was the female pseudonym of the author Algoth Untola, whose novel *Tulitikkuja lainaamassa* is set here; it is performed as a play in the town streets every summer. There's gorgeous natural scenery to be admired at ★ **Kypärävaara** on the hiking path between the villages of Riikola and Akkala, east of the Tohmajärvi–Kitee route.

The 490 road now travels through seemingly endless forest as it nears the Finno-Russian border. The amount of goods and people crossing the frontier at the town of **Värtsilä** (pop. 700), 80km (49 miles), has recently increased dramatically. Orthodox traditions are very much alive and well in this part of Karelia, as evidenced by such village edifices as the *tsasouna* (Orthodox village chapel with Byzantine architectural features) in **Mutalahti**, 130km (80 miles). The easternmost town in Finland, **Ilomantsi**, 150km (93 miles), is very Karelian indeed, and there's a permanent

Making music in Ilomantsi

Kalevala exhibition here. Nearby are also the oldest *tsasouna* (Orthodox chapel) in Finland: the ★ **Peter and Paul Chapel** in **Hattuvaara** (40km/24 miles northeast of Iilomantsi), and the **Church of St Elijah**, built in 1891.

Lieksa (pop. 15,000), 283km (175 miles), lies amid unspoilt natural scenery, and in terms of surface area is actually the second-largest population centre in the country. In **Vuonisjärvi**, roughly 15km (9 miles) outside Lieksa, the forest church and studio of the sculptress **Eva Ryynänen** (15 May to 15 September , 10am–6pm) are definitely worth a visit; her wood sculpture radiates a special warmth of its own. In Lieksa itself, the **Pielisen Museo** at Pappilantie 2 is Finland's best open-air museum, and gives a good idea of farm life spanning four centuries.

Those interested in a spot of canoeing or river-rafting should head eastwards from Lieksa to the ★★ **Ruunaa Rapids**, 30km (18 miles). There are six rapids to shoot in all, spread out across a distance of 31km (19 miles), and the whole procedure takes three to four hours.

57

Nurmes (pop. 10,000), 240km (149 miles), at the northwestern corner of Lake Pielinen, is famous for its birch trees. There's a charming Karelian village here with idyllic wooden houses and also the ★★ **Bomba House** (7am–10pm all year round; also has hotel and restaurant). It was built by the Russian Yegor Bomba and used to resemble a traditional family house from Sudjärvi in Soviet occupied Finnish Karelia (now the Karelian Republic in the Russian Federation). Torn down in 1934 and faithfully rebuilt in Nurmes, it has some fine Karelian wooden architecture and provides a good illustration of what life must have been like for an extended family of farmers in old Karelia.

Nurmes wooden house

Near Juuka, the Koli range of mountains comes into view, its peaks reflected in the waters of Lake Pielinen, Finland's sixth-largest lake. A few miles further on the ascent begins to the 347-m (1,138-ft) high ★★★ **Ukko-Koli**, 315km (195 miles), a peak that has inspired a great number of Finnish composers and writers. The view from the observation platform on the Ukko-Koli (the lift and the hotel up here are very unpopular with conservationists) down across the still waters of Lake Pielinen is one of the most stunningly memorable anywhere in Finland. There are hiking routes nearby to the peaks of **Akka-Koli** (339m/ 1,112ft) and **Paha-Koli** (334m/1,095ft).

Ukko-Koli provides inspiration

Returning to Joensuu, a nice way of finishing this trip is by taking a boat trip along the ★ **Jakokoski Museum Canal** (15 June to 15 August 10am–8pm, museum 14 June to 15 August, Tueday to Sunday noon–7pm). With its buildings, sluices, steamship and 'open-air canal theatre', it is a good way to learn about Finland's inland waterways.

Jakokoski Museum Canal

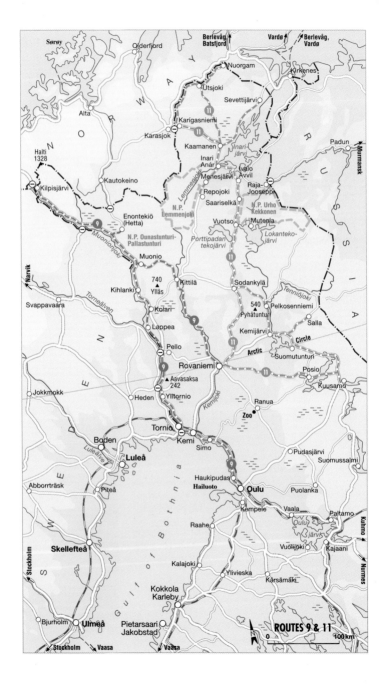

Sørøy   Olderfjord   Berlevåg,   Vardø   Berlevåg,
                     Batsfjord   Vardø

N   Nuorgam   Kirkenes

O   R   W   A   Y   Utsjoki

Alta   Sevettijärvi

                          Karigasniemi   11

Halti   Karasjok   11
1328
N   Kaamanen   Padun
                                    Inari-
Kilpisjärvi   Kautokeino   Inari   järvi   Murmansk
                          Anár
                                    Ivalo
              Enontekiö   Menesjärvi   Avvil
              (Hetta)   Repojoki   Raja-
                                       Jooseppi
          9   N.P.   Saariselkä   N.P. Urho
              Muonionjoki Lemmenjoki   Kekkonen

N.P. Ounastunturi-   Vuotso   Mutenia
Pallastunturi   Porttipadan   Lokanteko-
              Muonio   tekojärvi   järvi

Narvik   740   Kittilä   Sodankylä
          Kihlanki   Ylläs   Tenniöjoki
Svappavaara   540   Pelkosenniemi
              Kolari   Pyhätunturi
              Lappea   9   Salla
                          Kemijärvi
Tornealven   Pello   11   Arctic   Circle
          9   Rovaniemi   Suomutunturi

Jokkmokk   Aavasaksa 11   Posio
              242
          Heden   Ylitornio   Kuusamo
                          Kemijoki
                          Ranua
Boden   Tornio   Zoo
Luleå   Kemi   Simo
Luleälven
Abborrträsk   Piteå   Pudasjärvi   Suomussalmi

                  Haukipudas
          B   Hailuoto   9   Oulu   Puolanka
          o   Kempele   Vaala
          t   Raahe   Paltamo
Skellefteå t   Oulu-
          h   Vuolijoki   järvi   Kajaani
          n   Kalajoki   Kuhmo
          i   Ylivieska   Kärsämäki   Nurmes
          a
Stockholm S   Kokkola
                  Karleby
Bjurholm Umeå   Pietarsaari   ROUTES 9 & 11
                 Jakobstad
Stockholm   Vaasa   Vaasa   0   100km

Route 9

The Fells of Northern Finland *See map opposite*

Kokkola – Raahe – Oulu – Kemi – Tornio – Kukko-lankoski – Pello – Muonio – Kilpisjärvi – Enontekiö (Hetta) – Kittilä – Rovaniemi – Ranua – Oulu (1,645km/1,011 miles). *Note: mileage given beside a town name represents how far along the route it is.*

This five-day-long car or camper route (1,645km/1,011 miles, including 203km/126 miles to get to the starting-point from Kokkola) leads from Oulu along the coast and then along rivers next to the border, as far as the junction of Norway, Sweden and Finland. There are several places to stop and take a closer look at the fell country.

Oulu can be reached from south of Kokkola *(see Route 5, page 45)*: pass the ★ **Kalajoki Sandbanks** and then cross the coastal plain as far as **Raahe** (pop. 17,000), 108km (67 miles). Despite a serious fire in 1810 that devastated part of the town, several interesting sections still survive. Raahe's ★ **Pekkatori Marketplace** is considered the finest in the north. Strolling through the idyllic streets here you'd never believe that Raahe is also the site of the largest steelworks in all Scandinavia, the Rautaruukki.

Oulu (Uleaborg, pop. 123,000, www.oulutourism.fi), 203km (126 miles) was founded in 1605, and first became prosperous from exporting tar extracted from timber. Today the town is famous for its university and its microchip industries. Those keen on the wonders of modern science should visit the ★ **Tietomaa Science Centre** at Nahkatehtaankatu 6 (open all year round, 10am–4pm; in summer 10am–6pm; in July 10am–8pm). Its approach

Oulu has many attractions

59

Public art

Oulu town centre

Visitors to Hailuoto

The Sampo is based at Kemi

Tornio's wooden church

to technology is often entertaining. In mid-July the whole town and especially the ★ **Rotuaari**, its central pedestrian precinct, are filled with the aroma of fresh garlic, during the ritual celebration of 'Vampire Night'. Architectural sights of Oulu include the **Cathedral** (1832, CL Engel), the **Museum of Northern Ostrobothnia** (Monday to Thursday 8am–7pm, Saturday to Sunday, 11am–5pm) on the island of Ainola and the adjacent **Museum of Art** (Tuesday, Thursday, Friday 11am–6pm, Wednesday 11am–8pm, Saturday and Sunday 11am–6pm). The **marketplace** and **market hall**, situated to the west of the town centre, also contain several mouth-watering specialities. A good excursion from here is a trip to ★ **Hailuoto Island Bird Sanctuary**, 30km (18 miles); the car ferry is free of charge.

Passing small villages such as Haukipudas, and also the wild and beautiful Simojoki river, the route takes you to **Kemi** (pop. 23,400, www.kemi.fi), 335km (208 miles), where huge masses of floating logs can be seen awaiting further transportation or processing. In the summertime the icebreaker ★ *Sampo* can be visited in Ajos harbour (mid-May to mid- August daily 11am–8pm), with its café and restaurant. In the winter it cuts its way through Europe's largest ice fields, and has room on board for up to 150 passengers; the trip takes between 2 and 6 hours. For a different experience entirely, visit Kemi's ★ **Precious Stone Gallery** (Monday to Friday 8am–7pm, in summer also Saturday and Sunday 10am–6pm).

The town of **Tornio** (Torneå, pop. 22,500), 370km (229 miles), marks the southernmost point of the peaceful border between Finland and Sweden. It was founded in 1621 as a trading post on Suansaari Island, and seems almost a part of the neighbouring Swedish town of Haparanda; there are hardly any border checks. One interesting fact worth bearing in mind, however, is that there's a time difference of one hour between Sweden and Finland – a lot of watch-resetting goes on in Tornio. **Tornio Golf Club** is the oddest in Europe. During a round of 18 holes, you play nine in Sweden and nine in Finland – and there's one hour time difference between the two. It is a rare delight to play a night round in summer, thanks to the Midnight Sun.

The delta of the Tornio river, rich in salmon, gives a good foretaste of Lapland's wild beauty. Two sights definitely worth seeing here are the **Museum of Art** (Torikatu 2, Tuesday to Thursday, 11am–6pm; Friday to Sunday 11am–3pm) and the ★★ **wooden church** (summer Monday to Friday 9am–5pm), which dates from 1686. With its separate bell tower, it is considered to be one of the most beautiful in Finland. On a fine day, the best place to get a sense of town and surroundings is the observation platform on top of the water tower.

As far as excursions outside the town are concerned, one very fine sight 15km (9 miles) to the north of Tornio is **Kukkolankoski**, Finland's longest free-flowing rapids; the water plunges a full 14m (45ft).

The main attraction of **Ylitornio**, 440km (273 miles) is a hike up Mount Aavasaksa. At Juosenki we've reached the Arctic Circle – certificates immortalising the fact are available in Tuomaan Paja. The border town of **Pello** (pop. 4,700), 493km (306 miles), is very popular with anglers because of the Tornionjoki river and nearby Lake Miekojärvi (30km/18 miles southeast of Pello). There are some interesting craft shops, a good-value restaurant and also a fine view at ★ **Vihreä Pysäkki**, a popular excursion destination on the border bridge.

Kukkolankoski rapids

The route now continues northwards along the small road that runs alongside the Tornionjoki; near **Lappea**, the waterfalls mark the river's confluence with the Muonionjoki. The next major community back on the main road is **Kolari**, 569km (353 miles). This border municipality is actually made up of two smaller communities: **Yllasjärvi** (30km/18 miles), at the foot of the Ylläs Fell, and **Äkäslompolo** (27km/16 miles), on its northern slope and famous for its open-air Riekko Opera Festival during the summer months.

61

Just beyond the small community of Kihlanki (40km/24 miles before Mounio), a well-signposted forest path leads eastwards to Lake Pakasaivo *(see page 8)*, also known as 'The Hell of Lapland'. The lake was once a Same sacrificial site; offerings were made to the devil *(Piru)* they believed resided here. The water is at least 90m (295ft) deep, and is fed by subterranean springs.

The Midnight Sun at Ylitornio

River rafting from Muonio

The route continues now via **Muonio** (pop. 2,500), 644km (400 miles), a good starting-point for river-rafting expeditions, and then onwards towards Kilpisjärvi. Across to the east, round-topped fells reaching a maximum elevation of 500m (1,640ft) accompany the route. Finnish fells always seem to appear out of nowhere. The valleys and ravines here are typical of Lapland, as are the areas of moorland. The Midnight Sun shines in **Kilpisjärvi**, 840km (521 miles), the most northwesterly town in Finland, from 25 May to 22 July; the lake of the same name lies 472m (1,548ft) below sea-level. Here at the point where Norway, Sweden and Finland all meet, several hiking paths branch off in the direction of each country. Finland's highest fell (Saana, 1,029m/3,375ft) lies on the border with Norway here, and its highest mountain (Mt Haltia, 1,328m/4,356ft) is situated slightly to the northeast.

Hiking where three countries meet

The route back again leads along the same road as far as Palojoensuu, where the 958 provides a detour to **Enontekiö** (pop. 2,100), 1,016km (620 miles). Here there's a fascinating area of high fell, with tiny pools and streams of crystal-clear water flowing away westwards to the Munionjoki and eastwards to the Ounasjoki. The village of **Hetta** (part of Enontekiö) is where the Same celebrate *Marianpäivät*, their annual folk festival connected with weddings, confirmations and baptisms.

From Enontekiö, it's possible to head southwest to two more fells, Ounastunturi (723m/2,372ft) and Pallastunturi (807m/2,647ft), both situated in the very large (500sq km/193sq miles) **Pallas-Ounastunturi National Park**; there are many well-marked hiking routes here, and one particularly rewarding route is the (60km/37 miles) hike across both fells to Lake Ounasjärvi and then back again. In Muonio, which can be reached from the national park either by side-roads or by the main route described above, the road branches off towards the large community of **Kittilä**, 1,261km (780 miles). Situated at the foot of **Levitunturi Fell**, this popular winter sports centre is also the ★ **birthplace** (daily 10am–6pm) of the Lapp painter Reidar Särestöniemi.

From Kittilä, drive back to Oulu via Rovaniemi *(see page 63)*, 1,412km (870 miles), and **Ranua** (pop. 5,000), 1,494km (920 miles). There's a popular **cloudberry market** at Ranua on the first weekend in August; in addition, the town also boasts the northernmost ★ **zoo** in the whole world, with over 60 different Arctic species.

Särestöniemi's birthplace

Those still eager to do some more exploring after all this can drive from Kittilä to Sodankylä and connect with Route 11 *(see page 65)*.

Route 10

Rovaniemi: Gateway to the Arctic – Santa Claus Village

The town of **Rovaniemi** (pop 36,000, www.rovaniemi.fi), the administrative centre of the province of Lapland, is situated just south of the Arctic Circle. Although it did not receive its civic charter until 1960, it was first settled in the 11th century and experienced its greatest period of expansion during the early years of the 19th century when the riches of the Lappish forests attracted traders, prospectors and adventurers.

In 1944 the Germans burnt down almost the entire town during their forced retreat. The new town, designed by Alvar Aalto, is based on a ground-plan resembling reindeer antlers.

Jätkänkynttilä Bridge

Sights

The walking tour of Rovaniemi described here (4km/2½ miles, 3 hours) begins at the confluence of the Kemijoki and the Ounasjoki. The rapids here are spanned by the recently built ★ **Jätkänkynttilä Bridge**; cross it and then head for the modern city centre with its plentiful supply of pubs, shops and hotels, and the **Sampo Keskus** shopping arcade.

The next stop on the route is the ★★ **Arktikum** (May to June daily 10am–6pm, July to August 9am–7pm, September to April Tuesday to Sunday 10am–6pm), a long, glassed-over tunnel, forming a connection between modern city life and the fascinating natural environment of the Arctic. The intriguing nature of this part of the world is superbly portrayed in the two museums which form this scientific research centre, built by Bonerup and Torup-Wade in 1992.

Inside the Arktikum

It's worth dropping in to the **Lauri Tuotteet Salesrooms** (Pohjalankatu 25) to have a look at their fascinating and unusual selection of Lappish wood and reindeer-antler products. Pass the **Museum of Art** (Lapinkävijäntie 4, Tuesday to Sunday noon–6pm) to reach the long drawn-out Hallituskatu, with Aalto's ★ **Administrative and Cultural Complex**, made up of Lappia House (a congress centre), the Municipal Library and the Town Hall. A massive rock monument between the buildings created in 1988 by Kain Tapper, *The Birth of the Mountains*, symbolises Lapland's resurrection after the destruction wrought by the war.

The Provincial Museum in the Lappia House provides an introduction to Lapland's flora and fauna, Same traditions and Rovaniemi's history, but visitors will get a better feel of bygone living

**ROUTE 10
ROVANIEMI**

0   300m

from the 19th-century farm buildings at the **Pöykkölä
Museum**, by the Kemi river 3km(2 miles) to the south
on road 78. Not far from the Lappia House is the **Protestant Church** (June to August 9am–9pm), built in 1950
and based on plans by Bertil Liljeqvist. In summertime,
a pleasant way of finishing off this tour of Rovaniemi is
to visit the 'Valdemari' restaurant next to the Jätkänkynttilä Bridge – a good place from which to enjoy the gentle Arctic day and the Midnight Sun. The nightlife here
is surprisingly good , too; there are several nightclubs
and discos.

Another good route for a stroll through Rovaniemi is to
follow the Jäämerentie as far as the **Ounasvaara Ski
Stadium**. There's snow half the year round up here, and
skiing competitions and events are held from November
right through to March. In winter, which is 'peak season'
in Rovaniemi, motor sledges glide across frozen rivers,
cross-country skiers head off along their illuminated trails
and ice-golfers can be seen searching for their 'white
greens'. There's a good chairlift connection up to the top
of the **Ounasvaara** with its magnificent view across the
river valleys and the town, covered in snow or bathed in
the golden rays of the Midnight Sun, depending on the
time of year. In summer the sled run is a good way of
getting back down to the valley again.

Take the sled run down

Excursion to Santa Claus Village

The ★★ **Santa Claus Village**, located on the Arctic Circle, lies roughly 8km (5 miles) to the north of Rovaniemi.
Over 600,000 tourists a year make the pilgrimage to Santa
Claus; the enormous craft village has all kinds of gifts and
souvenirs on sale, and they can all be posted from here
to arrive anywhere in the world in time for Christmas.

Santa Claus at home

Route 11

To Gold Rush Territory in deepest Lapland *See map, page 58*

Rovaniemi – Sodankylä – Tankavaara (Saariselkä) – Ivalo –Inari – Lemmenjoki – Kaamanen – Sevettijärvi – Karigasniemi –Utsjoki – Pelkosenniemi – Kemijärvi – Kuusamo – Posio – Rovaniemi (1,288km/790 miles). *Note: mileage beside a town name represents how far along the route it is.*

This route leads from Rovaniemi via the Arctic Highway to the extreme north of Finland, crossing the region that attracted thousands of gold prospectors in the 19th century. Without detours, the entire trip is 1,288km/790 miles long; if started from Kittilä *(see page 62)* it's around 100km (60 miles) shorter. Those with plenty of time can extend this five- to seven-day trip to include the various national parks and Same settlements along the way.

Cross the Arctic Circle 8km (5 miles) north of Rovaniemi *(see Rovaniemi, page 63)*. Before the turn-off at Lake Vikajärvi, the **Arctic Highway** leads along the edge of the Raudanjoki to **Sodankylä** (pop. 9,700), 123km (76 miles). The Midnight Sun Film Festival held here each year is a popular event in the international film business. There are also some pleasant fells nearby in the **Luosto** region. The scenery up here is very much determined by the time of year. In September the autumn colours are unbelievably beautiful; at the peak of summer, gently-rounded fells, swirling rivers and serene forests characterise the landscape. Lapland is definitely a place for hikers; tourism has made hardly any inroads into this visually spectacular part of Finland.

Café in Sodankylä

Before the road rises into the marshland area ahead, pay a quick visit to the **Vuotso Same Village** next to the Lokka Reservoir for an insight into the mysteries of reindeer-herding and also take the opportunity to buy genuine handmade Same products.

The Arctic Highway now passes the ★ **Urho Kekkonen, National Park**, the second-largest in Finland (2,530sq km/977sq miles). It has a varied landscape: fells in the north with deep valleys, steep rock walls and vast areas of scree; huge pine forests, and wild rivers rich in fish to the southeast; and endless moorland to the southwest.

Hiking in the National Park

In ★★ **Tankavaara**, 233km, there's a **Gold Museum** documenting the great Lapland Gold Rush that broke out in the 19th century. All kinds of unlikely characters came up here to stake their claims and sift the rivers for gold. Today,

A common encounter
Panning for gold

visitors can do the same themselves, and very often find the odd little nugget – the perfect souvenir. There's an international gold-panning festival here at the beginning of August each year, and championships are even held every two years.

The tree-line now recedes into the distance as the journey continues. Dwarf birch and stunted pine are the only features in an otherwise barren, tundra-like landscape. At Laniila, 263km (163 miles), the highest point the road reaches, a half-mile-long asphalt track leads up to the summit of the **Kaunispää** (438m/1,436ft). Laanilä still has around ten mines dating from Gold Rush days, and sometimes genuine prospectors can be seen hard at work. On the right-hand side of the road the Saariselkä holiday centre with its good hotels can be seen. Further north, **Ivalo** (Same: *Avvil*), 288km (178 miles), soon comes into view; it is the administrative centre of the province of Inari. Ivalo has been inhabited since 1760, and boasts the northernmost airport in Finland. There's also a turn-off from here leading to the northernmost border post at **Raja-Jooseppi**.

From Ivalo, carry on to **Inari** (Same: *Anar*, pop. 7,300), 327km (203 miles), situated at the mouth of the Juutuanjoki where it meets Lake Inari, the sacred lake of the Same. Lake Inari is the second-largest lake north of the Arctic Circle in the world; covered with ice from October until the beginning of June, it is up to 96m (314ft) deep and has a total surface area of 1,085sq km (419sq miles). There are water-bus connections to **Ukonkivi Island** in the middle of the lake. Reindeer bones and ancient pieces of jewellery were found in the caves and crevices on the island – sacrificial offerings to the Same god *Ukko* ('old man'). Valuable information on the Same culture can be obtained at Inari's **Same Museum** (June to September

Lake Inari

9am–10pm, other months: Tuesday to Sunday, 10am–5pm); exhibits here include a reconstructed 19th-century Same village containing several *tipis*. A hiking path (7km/4 miles) near the museum leads to the **wooden church** in the Pielpajärvi region; it dates from 1760 and is only used once a year, on Midsummer Day.

Same woman

There's a good excursion possibility at this point. Near Menesjärvi, 36km (22 miles) southwest of Inari, is the **Lemmenjoki National Park** (46km/28 miles along the 9551 road, or 20km/12 miles by motor-boat). Several gold prospectors tried their luck here too, during the 1940s. The Same village of **Menesjärvi**, on the shore of the lake of the same name, is also definitely worth a visit; there's a campsite here too.

Lemmenjoki National Park

Back on the main route again, a side-road near the small town of **Kaamanen**, 359km (223 miles), on the Kaamasjoki, leads to **Sevettijärvi** (Same: *Ceavetjärvi*, 104km/60 miles to the northeast). Russian Orthodox Skolt-Same moved here in 1943 from Suonikylä in Petsamo. The village community here was set up in 1949 by the Finnish state, and the population lives off reindeer herding.

67

The road continues to **Karigasniemi** and then follows along the banks of the Tenojoki as far as **Utsjoki** (Same: *Ohcejoka*, pop. 1,400), 527km (327 miles), the northernmost municipality in Finland, which also contains Finland's northernmost village, **Nuorgam** (a 47km/29 mile detour to the northeast). A new bridge now spans the Tenojoki here, and leads across to Norway. Although this region is far removed from everyday life and refreshingly different for most visitors, the harsh realities of existence in the far north are usually less obvious: high unemployment, depression, and the high degree of atmospheric pollution resulting from heavy industry located on the Kola Peninsula.

Tenojoki river

Travelling back from the northern tip, it's a good idea to take a break 30km/18 miles south of Utsjoki and discover **Kevo** – the largest nature reserve in Finland.

It's the same stretch of road back again now as far as Sodankylä, 842km (523 miles); turn off here along the 5 road to **Pelkosenniemi**, 894km (555 miles). Anyone taking a side-road a few miles south of Pelkosenniemi will be rewarded by some magnificent scenery from the 540-m (1,771-ft) high **Pyhätunturi Fell** (there's a chairlift service to the top). From here the journey continues southeastwards via **Kemijärvi** (pop. 10,200), 951km (590 miles), the northernmost town in Finland, situated at the junction of the 510-km (316-mile) long Kemijoki river and Lake Kemijärvi.

Images of Oulanka

Cross the scenically beautiful Salla region now; in Joutsijärvi it's possible to take a rewarding detour to the mountain village of Salla, high up on the Iso Pyhätunturi Fell near the Russian border. The main route continues further southwards, passing the 408-m (1,338-ft) high **Suomutunturi** on the right; across to the left is the **Oulanka National Park** (and also the winter sports resort of **Ruka**), bordering the Oulanka river.

The southernmost point on the route before arriving back in Rovaniemi is **Kuusamo** (pop. 17,700), 1,096km (670 miles), where the scenery is still very much that of Lapland, with tundra stretching as far as the eye can see in any direction. The many lakes and fells in this marvellous wilderness country have made it especially popular with hikers, canoeists, anglers and hunters. One particularly good hiking trip follows the course of the so-called 'Bear Route' (75km/46 miles, 4–6 days), passing the impressive rock landscape near **Ristikallio**, the seething rapids of the **Taivalköngäs** and the mysterious **Oulanka Canyon**. Tours of the wilderness around Kuusamo are organised by several local operators; river rafting is also available. Winter sports enthusiasts will find the **Rukatunturi Skiing Centre** (462m/1,515ft) ideal.

In Nissinvaara, 10km (6 miles) to the north of Kuusamo, the main road leads on to **Posio**, 1,155km (710 miles), with its interesting **Pentik** ceramics factory (and sales floor) and its rather more unusual **Coffee Cup Museum** (summer 9am–8pm, Saturday 9am–6pm). The route then continues on from here back to Rovaniemi.

Anyone feeling up to it can miss out on Kuusamo and instead carry on further southwards via Kajaani, Sotkamo and Kuhmo as far as Iisalmi *(see Route 6, page 49)*.

Kuusamo is wilderness country

Route 12

Åland-hopping. *See map below. Note: mileage beside a town name represents how far along the route it is.*

This route explores the little-known Åland Islands, situated between Sweden and the southwest coast of Finland. There are over 6,000 of them, though only around five or six are inhabited, and even though the islands belong to Finland, everyone speaks Swedish. The roads through the archipelago pass some magnificent natural scenery, and this route is continuously – and very pleasantly – interrupted by embankments, bridges and ferries. The best way to get around is actually by bicycle – the Åland Islands even have special ferries just for cyclists – though car and especially boat would be viable alternatives. You can either bring your own bike or rent one.

Åland colours

The route – which has an optional extension incorporating the islands of Föglö and Kökar – crosses gently sloping countryside and plains, taking between five and six days to complete; its full length can't be measured exactly (between 100km/60 miles and 200km/124 miles) because it involves almost as much travel by sea as by land.

69

Always try keep a copy of the ferry timetable handy during this trip. Accommodation can generally be found without prior reservation: in hikers' huts, comfortable inns and boarding houses. There are also lots of campsites dotted across the islands. Another possibility is to book a 'bicycle package' holiday, though that means sticking to a

Travelling by boat

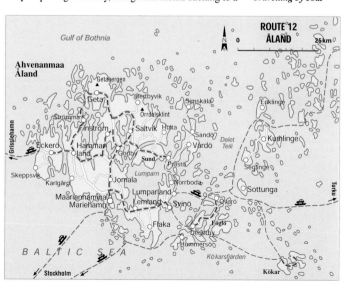

A craggy coast

route plan and particular places to stay. Simply cycling into the wild blue yonder is a fantastic feeling. With the islands' capital, Mariehamn, far behind, you're on your own with the beeches and birches, green meadows, colourful cows, windmills and dark-red houses with flagpoles in their gardens flying the islands' flag: a red-and-yellow cross on a blue background.

Though subject to Finnish sovereignty, the Åland Islands enjoy a large degree of autonomy. They have their own provincial parliament *(lagting)* with legislative powers, especially in cultural and economic matters, their own government, freedom from conscription, and also their own flag (since 1954). This dates back to the League of Nations: in 1921 Finnish sovereignty was established in return for autonomy and complete demilitarisation, and so the currency is the euro but the language is Swedish.

Mariehamn

Every second person on the Åland Islands lives in the capital, **Mariehamn** (Finnish: Maarianhamina, pop. 10,600, www.goaland.net). The town is jammed between two peninsulas – its east and west harbours respectively – and occupies the roughly mile-wide strip in the middle. The harbours are connected by the magnificent boulevard known as Norra Esplanadgatan; the highest buildings are those of the parliament at the west harbour and of the marine academy at the eastern one.

The town's name dates from the Russian interlude which lasted around a century from 1809: Tsar Alexander II founded the island's capital and named it after his wife, Maria. The islanders are famed for their combination of patriotism and cosmopolitanism. They have always been excellent mariners, and the islands once had the world's largest fleet of wooden sailing ships. Shipping is still the most important source of income: almost 60 percent of Finnish maritime trade operates from the Åland Islands.

The statue of the mariner next to the ★★ **Maritime Museum** in Mariehamn (daily 10am–4pm; May, June, August 9am–5pm; July 9am–7pm) stands in memory of all those who never returned. There are several nostalgic exhibits: sections of ship, captain's cabins, etc. Moored outside the museum is the four-masted ★★ *Pommern* (May to August 9am–5pm; July 9am–7pm; October 10am–4pm), built in Hamburg; now a museum ship, it once used to carry freight between Australia and England. Don't miss the excellent **Åland Museum** either in the Stadhusparken, which documents the fascinating history of the islands. Many Roman coins have been found, along with numerous Viking burial mounds (daily May to August 10am–4pm, Tuesday until 8pm; September to April Tuesday to Sunday 11am–4pm, Tuesday also 6–8pm).

The Pommern can be visited

Åland Museum

Apart from several excellent pubs and cafés, highlights of Mariehamn include the ★ **Ålandspark** recreation area on **Lilla Holmen**, a small island with a beach, and also **Grönä Udden** (green headland), the town's most popular place for a swim.

Lemland's 13th-century church

71

Mariehamn – Jomala – Lemland – Lumparland

Now leave the 'big city' behind. Cyclists should keep an eye out for the green-and-white signs, placed here specifically for them. Take the 3 road in an easterly direction. After a few miles across some very pretty landscape, the **Lemström Canal**, which separates Jomala from Lemland, comes into view; it was built in 1882 and is only a few hundred yards long.

At the side of the road, the ★ **Onningeby Museum** (7 June to 22 August daily 10am–4pm, Thursday also 6–9pm) contains several works of art inspired by the islands' landscape, many of them the work of women painters. Much of the scenery is recognisably that of the Åland Islands – especially in the paintings of the **Ramsholmen** nature conservation area on Jomala.

Farm on Jomala

On Lemland there's a 13th-century **church** that is definitely worth a visit, like all the churches on the Åland Islands, with their rough-carved natural stone exteriors, set against the green-and-blue island scenery. The frescoes inside this church are very fine. The islands were converted to Christianity at the beginning of the 11th century, and were incorporated into the bishop's see of Åbo (Turku) during the 13th century when they became part of the Kingdom of Sweden. The medieval churches on the islands are thus the legacy of Swedish immigrants.

The roads on Lumparland all end at ferry harbours. From **Svinö**, the southernmost point, there's a ferry connection to Föglö; **Långnäs** at the eastern end has ferries to Kökar and Kumlinge, and also to Sund.

Quayside capers

Föglö and Kökar

Bicycles just whizz along here across the flat plains, past fishing boats, anglers, boat-houses, frightened eider ducks and wild swans. **Föglö** is very much a fishing island, and a paradise for anglers: pike, trout, salmon and Baltic herring are just a few of the delicious fish to be caught here.

The island of **Kökar** has hardly any trees, but to make up for that there's a Franciscan monastery and an artists' colony. The island ferry takes 2 hours to get back to Lumparland from here, and there's a further connection via bicycle ferry to Sund.

The 'Mainland' Region

The islands connected by bridges skirting the water, ie the main island with Mariehamn, and Eckerö, to the west, and Lemland and Lumparland to the southeast, are referred to collectively by the locals as Fasta Åland (the mainland).

Fortress of Castelholm

On **Sund**, the ★★ **Fortress of Castelholm** (May to mid-August 10am–5pm), first mentioned in 1388, has been painstakingly restored. It was built by the Swedes to consolidate their domination of the Baltic. King Gustav Vasa and several other crowned heads of Sweden once played in its rooms as children.

The ruins at Bomarsund

The ruins of the fortress of ★ **Bomarsund** are 12km (7 miles) to the east. This Russian castle wasn't even completed when it was blown up by an Anglo-French force in 1854 during the Crimean War. Today the ramparts are all that remain. Sund's **Church of St John the Baptist** is definitely worth a visit. There's a superb view across the island landscape from this large medieval building; the interior contains a cross in memory of the Bremen archbishop Wenni, who died on Sund during the 10th century while on his way to convert heathens in Scythia.

Postbox on Saltvik

The route to **Saltvik**, an island rich in history and famous for its archaeological finds, winds its way over slopes and alongside forests as far as the **Church of St Mary**; the square in front was where the local parliament used to assemble. The **Orrdalsklint** is 128m (419ft) above sea level – the highest 'peak' on the Åland Islands. There's a fantastic view from the top. The village of **Långbergsoda** at the foot of the hill is a good place to park the bicycle and visit the Stone Age settlement. Ancient finds here prove that the Åland Islands were inhabited over 6,000 years ago. A significant amount of immigration took place around AD600 – the fertile islands were an attractive prospect for herdsmen. The Viking burial mounds date from the period during which the islands were converted to Christianity – at that time they were the most densely populated area of northern Europe – and the islanders proudly regard them as part of their heritage.

Visit the second-highest mountain on the islands now, **Mount Geta**. Its cliff dropping down to the water's edge fascinates geologists and also visitors to the **Soltuna** tourist station at the top: a great place to spend the night in the open air and enjoy the moonscape above the islands.

After a 20-minute trip on the bicycle ferry, the journey continues across undulating countryside to **Hammarland**. The River Marsund, spanned by an arched bridge on the way to Eckerö, is particularly rich in fish. Hammarland's **Church of St Catherine** is rather forbidding.

At the end of the paved section of road is **Eckerö**, which consists of one main island (pop. 7,500) and 200 smaller ones; it's the westernmost municipality of the Åland Islands, and thus of Finland as a whole. The striking yellow ★ **post office** can be seen above the smooth rocks; it was built in the Empire style by CL Engel on the order of Tsar Alexander I, who wanted to impress the Swedes with a magnificent piece of architecture. Eckerö was important for the postal system in those days: from 1636 to 1898 boats full of mail plied regularly between here and Roslage in Sweden. An annual 'post boat competition' between Eckerö and Grisslehamn is still held in June.

Around 11km (6 miles) outside Mariehamn, the hills of **Ingby** contain Bronze Age tombs. Around a mile further on towards Mariehamn, behind some tall trees, one of the oldest stone churches in Northern Europe can be seen: Jomala's **Church of St Olaf**. It was built around 900 years ago and was also used for defensive purposes.

Back in Mariehamn, now is a good time to buy some souvenirs. Ceramic goods, Åland Island wool in the national colours, and wonderfully carved wooden containers traditionally used for storing pickled herring are just a few of the items available. Most shops in Mariehamn and on the islands as a whole are also open on Sunday.

Getting ready to sail
The post office

Finish off with a barbecue

Art History

Architecture

Finish architecture is as young as the nation itself. Only very few stone buildings, medieval castles and churches have survived, and much of the wooden architecture of the 17th and 18th century (including entire city centres) has long since fallen victim to fire. This makes the areas of wooden housing that still survive – such as Rauma's old town with 600 or so buildings dating from the 18th and 19th century – all the more precious.

The foundations for the country's new direction in architecture were laid by Carl Ludwig Engel (1778–1840), a German architect from Berlin working in Finland. CL Engel was responsible for giving the young capital city of Helsinki its classical face; one of his greatest achievements was the magnificent Senate Square.

Finland's growing national consciousness exerted a very strong influence on local architects, and laid the foundations for the later international fame of Finnish architecture. At the turn of the 20th century architects such as Eliel Saarinen (1873–1930) and Lars Sonck (1870–1956) combined construction materials such as medieval flint and Karelian wood to create a special Finnish art nouveau. Saarinen designed Helsinki's National Museum and also the much-admired Finnish Pavilion at the international exhibition in Paris in 1900, on which he collaborated with Armas Lindgren and Herman Gesellius. These three architects constructed several magnificent buildings together, including Hvitträsk in Kirkkonummi (Espoo).

At the beginning of the 1920s a classical-rational style developed; the most striking example of it is perhaps Helsinki's Parliament Building, designed by JS Siren (1889–1961). The negative side of this style resulted in several over-life-sized statues in honour of the 'Finnish Heroes of the Present'; one such example is the *Old Men* statue outside Siren's Parliament Building.

Meanwhile, Functionalism was beginning to establish itself, and Finland's most celebrated architect, Alvar Aalto (1898–1976), created its first monument with his design for the tuberculosis sanatorium in Paimio. His Finnish Pavilion for the 1939 New York World Fair brought him international recognition; from then on he designed buildings all over the world. In Finland he built residential areas, schools, universities, administration buildings, theatres and industrial installations. Helsinki's Finlandia Hall was built during Aalto's final 'white' period.

The grand old man of Finnish architecture, Aalto, provided inspiration for many young and individualistic architects. Buildings that have won international acclaim include The Townhouse in Toronto designed by Viljo

Opposite: Helsinki Cathedral, designed by Engel

Wooden houses in Porvoo

Door design by Alvar Aalto

Rewell (1910–64), the Kaleva Church in Tampere (1966) by Reima Pietilä, the 'Rock Church' in Helsinki by Timo and Tuomo Suomalainen, and Tampere's Municipal Library, designed by Reima and Raili Pietilä.

Craftsmanship and design

The term 'Finnish design', whether in the sphere of craft or industry, has come to mean functionality, clear and harmonious lines and colour combinations, and the careful use of local natural materials. The earliest 'Finnish designers' were architects like Eliel Saarinen and Alvar Aalto, whose furniture and lamps are now considered classics of their time. Ever since Finnish design made its international breakthrough at the Milan Triennale during the 1950s, star designers like Tapio Wirkkala and Timo Sarpeneva (glass), Dora Jung (textiles) and Bertel Gardberg (metal and jewellery) have firmly established Finland's international reputation. In the world market the design style is exemplified by brand names such as Marimekko (textiles), Arabia (porcelain and ceramics), Iittala (glass), and Riihimäki and Kumela (shoes and furs). Finnish jewellery has only been exported during the past 30 years or so despite its 600-year-old history. Meanwhile, Kalevala jewellery based on old designs has become just as popular on the world market as has Björn Weckström's striking *Lapponia* jewellery.

Some of Aalto's classic furniture

Fine arts

Orthodox panel, Kuopio

Medieval painting in Finland's grey stone churches often betrays a clear Central European influence. Many works by early masters on the walls of wooden churches were destroyed by fire. In the mid-19th century the 'Düsseldorf School' provided several Finnish painters with inspiration, which they gradually developed into their own style. The work of the greatest artist of this period, Albert Edelfelt (1854–1905), was still very much influenced by the Italian and French painting styles.

The national style created by Akseli Gallen-Kallela (1865–1931) was so popular that most Finnish artists painting around the turn of the 20th century largely ignored influences from Central and Southern Europe. Finland's greatest Expressionist painter Tyko Sallinen (1879–1955) was followed by several more young Expressionist artists, many of whom set new standards. In contrast to Sallinen's rather stubborn subjectivity, the sensitive portraits of women by Helene Schjerfbeck (1862–1946) reduced expression to its bare essentials.

Finnish sculpture also found its own voice rather late, experiencing its greatest popularity just after the end of World War II. Memorials had to be built, new residential areas needed sculpture work, and much of this was ex-

Lapp art by Reidar Särestöniemi

ecuted by Wäino Aaltonen (1894–1966). He used granite, marble, copper and bronze in his work, which set new standards in the medium (eg the Hämeensilta Bridge at Tampere). The war memorials created by Aimo Tukiainen reveal a transition from realistic to abstract sculpture (eg his 1960 equestrian statue of Marshal Mannerheim in Helsinki). For most visitors to Helsinki, the massive *Sibelius Monument* by the Finnish sculptress Eila Hiltunen (1960) is hard to miss. Several other sculptors work with wood, eg Kain Tapper, Mano Hartmann and Martti Aiha; their work often betrays a compelling affinity with nature.

An Aaltonen bronze

Literature

The earliest examples of written Finnish are the first translation of the Bible (1545) and also Mikael Agricola's translation of the New Testament (1548), but it was only in the 19th century that Finland's writers began to use their own language rather than Swedish, although with his stories of life in the 17th and 18th centuries, published as *The Surgeon's Stories (Fältskärns berättelten*, 1851–60), Zacharias Sakari Topelius (1818–98), who wrote in Swedish, is actually regarded as the father of the Finnish historical novel.

Topelius's house

The year 1835 saw the publication of the *Kalevala*, the epic which lies at the very heart of Finnish culture. It was compiled by the scholar Elias Lönnrot (1802–84) from ancient Finnish ballads, incantations and lyrics, and together with *Seven Brothers (Seitsemän veljestä)* by Aleksis Kivi (1834–72) it played a vital role in fostering Finnish national consciousness. Kivi's work was the first proper Finnish novel set in Finland; its mixture of realism and humour created a national literary style.

The theme of failure runs right through Finnish literature, appearing in the work of Finland's only literary Nobel prizewinner, FE Sillanpää (1888–1964), who was awarded the prize in 1939. The changing relationship between national and individual destiny is explored by the country's post-war authors such as Väinö Linna (1920–92), whose novels dwell on war, loss of land and refugee problems. Linna's main work, *The Unknown Soldier (Tuntematon sotilas)*, an account of the cynical, brutal side of war, was also made into a famous film. The historical novels by Mika Waltari (1908–79) have also sold millions.

Contemporary writers such as Paavo Haavikko *(King Harald)*, Veijo Meri *(Quits)* and the Swedish-language authoress Märta Tikkanen *(How to Rape a Man)* have taken a social-critical standpoint much influenced by city life.

One famous Swedish-language authoress who was born in Helsinki in 1914 was Tove Jansson. She created the fantastic, self-contained world of the *Moomintrolls*. The books are a pleasure for all ages.

Theatre, Music and Film

The Finns love theatre: Finland has 40 established theatres, innumerable amateur and semi-professional dramatic groups and capacity audiences. Finnish drama only began 120 years ago, however, with the first performance of *Leah* by Aleksis Kivi. Style and expression now ranges from social-critical work to the classic national theatre, which features many high-budget performances of works by Brecht and Chekhov.

Finnish film-making has been attracting international attention, particularly the work of the brothers Aki and Mika Kaurismäki. Their films, such as Aki's *The Man Without a Past* (which won the Grand Prix at Canes in 2002) are very poetic and contain hardly any dialogue; they tell of uprooted existences, and of unsuccessful returns to seemingly idyllic rural surroundings.

Music

The oldest melodies in Finland – folk tales and laments – were transmitted orally, and church music was preserved from the 13th century. Much of the early medieval folk poetry in the *Kalevala* was originally sung to the accompaniment of the five-stringed zither known as the *kantele*.

Folk musician

Sibelius looms large

The most important Finnish composer is without a doubt Jean Sibelius (1865–1957). His early works and symphonies (such as the five-section *Kullervo*) used material and motifs from the *Kalevala*; his seven great symphonies, his violin concerto, his *Karelia Suite* and his symphonic poem *Finlandia* were all inspired by national themes. The music scene in Finland went very quiet after Sibelius, and new shoots seem only to have appeared during the last two decades, all of them reflecting international trends. The opera *Juha* by Aarne Merikanto is set in Karelia. Famous contemporary composers include Erik Bergmann, Joonas Kokkonen and Aulis Sallinen, whose opera *Kullervo* is based on the tragedy of the same name by Aleksis Kivi; it takes an apocalyptic look at today's gradual erosion of Finnish culture.

There are several famous Finns active in the international music scene. Famous Finnish conductors include Esa Pekka Salonen, Leif Segerstam and Jukka-Pekka Saraste. Aulikki Rautavaara, Anita Välkki, Taru Valjakka and Tamara Lund are all well-known female opera singers, and their celebrated male counterparts include Kim Borg, Tom Krause, Matti Salminen and Walton Grönroos.

Classical music in Finland revolves around the Finnish National Opera, Helsinki's Finlandia Hall and the Savonlinna International Opera Festival. Other major international music events such as the annual jazz festival in Pori attract musicians and fans from all over the world.

Festivals & Folklore

The moment the summer comes, the Finns head for the countryside. And since the summers in Finland are short, the twilight months are one big festival. The most important summer festivals – of which there are 50 or more – are referred to collectively as the 'Finland Festival'. These range from chamber music in the village church in Kuhmo to the Film Festival in Sodankylä. There are jazz festivals in Pori, Tornio and Kainuu, and also the famous Festival of Dance and Music in Kuopio. Another popular event is the Opera Festival in Savonlinna. At the end of the summer activity returns to the larger cities. The Helsinki Festival is held at the end of August.

Here is a list of the more important annual events:

6 January: *Loppiainen*, door-to-door carol-singing.
Seven weeks before Easter: *Laskiaisunnuntai*, ski carnival with accompanying events.
Last weekend in February: *Finlandia-hiihto*, 75-km (46-mile) skiing trip between Hämeenlinna and Lahti.
March: Ski trips from border to border.
Two weeks before Easter: *Marianpäivät*, festival of the Same in Hetta.
Second week in March: International Film Festival in Tampere.
Easter: Festival of the Skolt Lapps in Sevettijärvi.
1 May: *Vappu* Festival.
Second–third week in June: Finland Festival, including Midnight Sun Film Festival in Sodankylä, Festival of Dance and Music in Kuopio, music festivals in Ilmajoki and Naantali, Chamber Music Festival in Korsholm, concerts in Riihimäki, and Jyväskylä Summer Festival.
20–26 June: Midsummer Night festivals on the Friday and Saturday of this week; bonfires and dancing.
Second week in July: Seinäjoki Tango Market, the biggest tango music festival in the world.
July to the beginning of August: Savonlinna International Opera Festival.
Second–third week in July: Jazz Festival in Pori.
Last two weeks in July: Chamber Music Festival in Kuhmo.
Last week in July: Brass band Festival in Lieksa.
Second–third week in August: Turku Music Festival.
Second week in August: Tampere International Theatre Festival.
End of August/Early September: Helsinki Festival.
First weekend in November: Tampere Jazz Happening.
Third week in November: International Children's Film Festival in Oulu.

Midsummer Festival, Helsinki

Food and Drink

Finnish food isn't an everyday topic of conversation in Central Europe, but what to eat where and when is an important question on any trip through Finland. The most inexpensive course of action is to catch a fish and cook it over an open fire – though you do need a local fishing permit first. Another quick meal – ideal after the sauna for instance – is Finnish sausage *(lenkkimakkara)*. Beware, though: they can be very fatty and are one of the reasons why Finland once had such a high level of heart disease.

A far more exclusive pleasure is marinated salmon *(graavi lohi)* and marinated rainbow trout *(graavi kirjolohi)*. Trout in particular is unforgettably delicious, especially when smoked out-of-doors over a fire.

Buffet platters

A lot of visitors arrive by ship and their first contact with Finnish food is via the Scandinavian buffet on board; this resurfaces in Finland under the name *seisova pöytä*. The best way to tackle the buffet is to start with rollmop herring, then go on to fish and seafood and eat the meat dishes (which may include roast reindeer) last. Side-dishes invariably include fresh salad, mushrooms and delicious small potatoes. Cheese and fruit round off the meal.

81

Genuine Finnish food can only really be experienced if you are lucky enough to be invited into a Finnish home. Sausage and fried dumplings are high on the list of family favourites. Soufflés tend to be served around Christmas time, and soups of all kinds are extremely popular. Pea soup is delicious in Finland, and the summer soup known as *kesäkeitto* filled with herbs and vegetables is also surprisingly good; the fish soups are quite superb.

Finnish people like to serve up delicious small pancakes known as *lätty*, and a bowl of fruit called *kiiseli* often tends to arrive for pudding. It's a real honour in Finland to be invited to eat a tender, juicy elk steak.

Typical regional dishes in eastern Finland include *karjalanpaisti* and *karjalan piirakat*; the former is a substantial meat stew containing beef, mutton and pork, and the latter is a flat section of pastry filled with rice or creamed potato and served warm with butter and salt. *Kalakukko* is black bread with a fish and meat filling.

A culinary must on any trip to Finland is reindeer meat. It tastes particularly good chopped up in a cream sauce *(poronkäristys)*, or cold and smoked. Reindeer meat is exceptionally high in protein and low in fat.

Reindeer stew

There's one gastronomic delight that should perhaps be placed in the 'sports' section of this guide: on 21 July each year the crayfish *(rapu)* season begins. The freshly-caught crayfish are flung into boiling water and brought to the table in an artistic pile festooned with dill. It's at this point that the custom known as 'crayfish drinking' commences.

Strawberry season

The world's smallest restaurant, Iisalmi

Anyone invited to a crayfish marathon usually joins in the fun, which consists of filling the empty crayfish carapaces with vodka and draining them with amazing rapidity.

Vodka is not only used for washing down crayfish. The high-grade Finnish variety is delicious with ice and is a very good way of thinning down the various local berry liqueurs. *Mesimarja* comes from Arctic raspberries, *lakka* from loganberries and *karpalo* from cranberries. The clear schnapps known as *koskenkorva* is best left to the locals.

Finland has now relaxed its strict rules governing the consumption of alcohol: beers and medium-strength wines are available now not only from state-run alcohol stores but also in grocery shops and supermarkets. The Finns' favourite drink, however, is coffee. They are Europe's number one consumer of the beverage. They drink coffee on almost any occasion, despite all advice to the contrary. Anyone who suddenly feels the need for a cup of coffee in Finland only needs to drive to the next petrol station where there is always an adjoining cafeteria. The food at these places is good value, too.

Restaurant Selection
These recommended restaurants can be found on the routes mentioned in this book. Prices fall within the following guidelines: €€€ = expensive, €€ = moderate and € = cheap.

Ekenäs (Tammisaari)
€€**Knipan**, Stallörsparken, tel: 019-241 1169.

Espoo
€€**Haikaranpesä**, Haukilahti Water Tower, tel: 09-452 4254. A great view.

Hamina
€**Marski Café**, Raathuoneentori 1, tel: 05-354 1600. Mixed guests.

Hanko
€€**Origo**, Satamakatu 7, tel: 019-248 5023. Varied fish buffet; €**Pirate**, Satauakatu 13, tel: 019-248 3006. A real pirates' den.

Heinola
€**Café-Restaurant Kestitupa**, Siltakatu 11, tel: 03-715 2288. Good food, quick service.

Helsinki
€€€**Lehtovaara**, Mechelininkatu 39, tel: 09-493 408. An import from Vyborg, very fine food. €€€**Lord Hotel**, Lönnrotinkatu 29, tel: 09-615815. The upstairs restaurant of this fine hotel serves excellent fish dishes; €€€**Restau-**

rant **Saslik**, Neitsytpolku 12, tel: 09-348 9700. Russian cuisine, sadly bear is also on the menu; **€€€Savoy**, Eteläesplanadi 14, tel: 09-176571. Finnish and international cuisine; **€€Kellarikrouvi**, Pohjoinen Makasiinikatu 6, tel: 09-179021. Substantial helpings of delicious Finnish food; **$$Konstan Mölja**, Hietalahdenkatu 15, tel: 09-694 7504. Memories of the old harbour near Vyborg and inexpensive all-you-can-eat buffets. **€€Silvoplee**, Toinen Linja 3, tel: 09-726 0900. An interesting vegetarian restaurant near Hakaniemi. **€€Zetor**, Mannerheimintie 3-5, tel: 09-666 966. A fun pub and restaurant with an incredible decor.

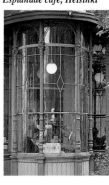

Esplanade café, Helsinki

Joensuu
€€Puukello, Ilosaari Island, tel: 013-123272. Karelian specialities.

Jyväskylä
€€Savutuvan Apaja, Vaajakoski, tel: 014-262022. Good home cooking.

Kaamanen
€Kaamasen Kievari, tel: 016-672713. Good home-cooked fare.

Kemi
€€€Hullunmylly, Raatihuoneenmäki, tel: 016-4580440.

Kotka
€€Fort Elisabeth, Varissaari Island, tel: 05-212766. Summer restaurant; **€€Kairo**, Satamakatu 7, tel: 05-212787. Nautical restaurant and a famous pub.

Kristiinankaupunki
€€Café Alma, in the marketplace, tel: 06-221 3455.

83

The Savoy, Helsinki

Laanila
€€Kammi, Saariselkä, tel: 016-667108. Lapp dishes.

Lahti
€€Oldi, Aleksanterinkatu 9, tel: 03-752 0066. In the marketplace, good for lunches; **€Penthouse**, Saimaankatu 29, tel: 03-781 7995. Cheap meals, central location.

Lappeenranta
€€Majakka, Satamatie 4, tel: 05-451 4835. Nostalgic atmosphere, close to the castle.

Lieksa
€€Kestikievari Herraniemi, 30km/19 miles out of Lieksa in Vuonislahti, tel: 013-542110. Good food and fast service.

Loviisa
€€Kievari Degerby Gille, Sepänkuja 4, tel: 019-50561; **€€€Degerby**, Brandensteininkatu 17, tel: 019-50561. Centrally located.

Mariehamn
€€Nautical, near the *Pommern*, tel: 018-19931. Fine sea views.

Mikkeli
€€Kenkävero, Pursialankatu 6, tel: 015-162245.

Naantali
€€Kala-Trappi, Nunnakatu 3, tel: 02-435 2477. Good seafood.

Oulu
€€Neptunus, Torinranta, tel: 08-372572. Inside an old sailing ship at the marketplace.

Making pancakes and smoking salmon

Pori
€€€Raatihuoneen Kellari, Hallituskatu 9, tel: 02-633 4804. First-class establishment in every way.

Porvoo
€€Wanha Laamanni, Vuorikatu 17, tel: 019-523 0455. Near the cathedral with nice view of old town.

Rovaniemi
€€€Fransmanni, Koskikatu 4, tel: 016-332211. The best restaurant in town.

Sund
€€Golfrestaurangen, Kastelholm, tel: 018-43828. Summer restaurant.

A fine Finnish dinner

Tampere
€€€Restaurant Astor, Aleksis Kivenkatu 26, tel: 03-213 3522. Relaxed atmosphere with live music. **€€€Tiiliholvi**, Kauppakatu 10, tel: 03-272 0231. Gourmet restaurant with a good wine list. **€€Salud**, Tuomio-kirkonkatu 19, tel: 03-366 4460. Spanish-style restaurant with rare game.

Tornio
€€Green Line Welcome Center, Pakkahuoneenkatu, tel: 016-431900. Restaurant with great views.

Turku
€€€Brahen Kellari, Puolalankatu 1, tel: 02-232 5400. Popular restaurant in a vaulted cellar – the bear here is delicious; **€€€Julia**, Eerikinkatu 4, tel: 02-336311. Award-winning restaurant in the Julia Hotel; imaginative cuisine with a French influence. **€€Harald**, Aurakatu 3, tel 02-276 5050. A rustic gourmet restaurant in the centre of Turku. **€Pinella**, Porthanin puisto, tel: 02-251 7557. 140 years of tradition, though only open in summer.

Uusikaupunki
€€Pryki, Vakka-Suomenkatu 19, tel: 02-841 5055. Summer terrace.

Vaasa
€€Gustav Wasa, Raastuvankatu, tel: 06-326 9200. Very friendly restaurant.

Vantaa
€€Chic, Kielotie 8, tel: 09-823 4832. Near Heureka Scientific Centre.

Varkaus
€€Keskushotelli, Ahlströminkatu 18, tel: 017-579011.

85

Active Holidays

Hikers in the Oulanka

Hiking and horse riding

The best way to discover Finland's natural scenery is to hike across it – or, in wintertime, to ski across it. Finland's 29 national parks are criss-crossed by a seemingly endless network of marked paths, nature trails and cross-country skiing routes. Camping and picnic sites are available everywhere. Those with no time for a hiking trip lasting several days should at least take a short guided tour through the Nuuksio wilderness, which is only half an hour's drive away from Helsinki.

Finland has very little in the way of mountains, except in the far north where some of the Lappish hills exceed 4,000ft (1,400m). In the south of the country, hikers will experience broad forests with numerous ponds and lakes. The landscape in central and eastern Finland gets increasingly barren as the lakes gradually give way to swamp and marshland. In Lapland the forest thins out and the landscape is stark and haunting. At the beginning of June the twilight nights are ideal for long hikes that can last well into the morning. A lot of hikers prefer September, however, when a sparkling layer of frost covers the magnificent autumn colours in preparation for the first snows.

Finland's forest are also ideal for excursions on horseback, which can last from only one hour to several days. A day trip on a comfortable Iceland pony costs about €75.

Winter wayfarers

Winter Sports

Winter is the high point of the year for sports in Finland. Cross-country skiing is extremely popular; there are also countless well-tended ski-runs, several of which are flood-lit. Unfortunately for the landscape, the Finns have developed a taste for Alpine skiing: every hill has ski-lifts and snowboard runs.

Skiers keen to go on cross-country skiing trips between November and February need to be physically fit. In March the sun is already starting to warm things up a bit, but April is the most popular month for skiing. In May, spring arrives in central and southern Finland, but there's still the chance to ski further north

Motor-sledge safaris, reindeer-drawn sleigh rides, ice-hole fishing, ice golf and excellent skating in the open air round off the range of winter attractions.

Cycling

Southern Finland is ideal for cycling tours. There is a comprehensive network of side-roads, many of which lead through remote villages; there's always somewhere to rest or go for a swim. The Åland Islands are also perfect for

Pedal power

a cycling holiday. Recent years have seen a boom in mountainbiking, and numerous routes have been developed.

Fishing and hunting

Finland's numerous lakes contain an almost inexhaustible supply of fish, and are ideal for hobby anglers. The areas where fishing is allowed are constantly monitored, however, and anglers over the age of 18 need two documents: a state permit *(kalastuskortti)*, which can be bought at any post office for about €14; and a fishing licence *(kalastuslupa)* from the owner of the waters in question generally the local tourist office, campsite or holiday centre. Most fishing areas in eastern and northern Finland are state-owned, and licences can be obtained from the local forestry offices.

Anglers need permits

Finland's waters are rich in pike, perch, whitefish and bream, and special sports fishing areas contain trout and salmon. Rivers famous for salmon are the Teno (on the border of Finland and Norway) and Tornionjoki (on the border of Finland and Sweden). The coastal waters of the Baltic, with their low salt content, also contain several varieties of freshwater fish, and flounder, pike and perch can all be caught offshore.

87

Hunting in Finland is only allowed at certain times of year and is very strictly controlled. Hunting rights are the privilege of landowners, who often lease out their land. In southern Finland hunters need a permit from the local landowner or hunting association; in eastern and northern Finland, hunting permits are issued by the forestry commission. Elk is popular – but tricky – game to hunt; wildfowl is easier with a good dog. The elk season begins in mid-October and ends between the end of November and the end of December, depending on the region.

Water sports

Enjoying the sun at Saarijärvi

Finland's vast network of lakes and rivers is ideal for water sports – and access to most of the islands and riverbanks is hardly ever prohibited. The Finns make the most of this natural arena, especially during the long days of summer, when they engage in sports such as river rafting in dinghies (and even wooden longboats), canoeing, windsurfing and sailing.

It's almost impossible to lose your way as a canoeist. Even the Saimaa, Europe's largest lake system, has 2,000km (1,240 miles) of clearly marked routes. All levels of skills are catered for, from easy paddling across lakes to hurtling down thundering rapids; the archipelagoes along the south and southwest coast are ideal for sea canoeing. For more information contact the Finnish Canoe Association, Olympic Stadium, Etelä Kaarre, Helsinki, tel: 09-494 965.

Getting There

By air

Finnair is the national carrier of Finland and operates both national and international routes. There are direct flights from all the major European cities including London, which has daily nonstop flights (2 hours 50 minutes) by Finnair and British Airways to Helsinki. Finnair, 14, Clifford Street, London W1X 2NS; tel: 020-7408 1222; British Airways, tel: 0345-222111. Finnair provides the only direct service between the US and Finland, flying daily from New York to Helsinki. Finnair, 228 East 45th Street, NY; tel: 212-499 9000.

Helsinki-Vantaa International Airport is connected by Finnair bus and local bus to Helsinki. There is also a taxi stand; traffic into the city is not usually a problem.

By train

It's a long haul to Finland from just about anywhere in Europe by rail, because the long rail trip north is inevitably followed by a 15-hour journey by boat and train from Stockholm to Helsinki. From Britain, the handiest route is Sealink from Harwich to the Hook of Holland and overland to Copenhagen, then connecting train to Stockholm and boat or boat and train to Turku or Helsinki. Total travel time is about 45 hours.

In Stockholm the subway *(tunnelbana)* or a taxi will take you to the ferry with connections to Turku (Värtahamnen/Silja Line or Tegelsvikhamnen/Viking Line). There are train connections to Helsinki, northeastern Finland and Lapland (Rovaniemi/Kemijärvi) from Turku harbour. Both shipping lines provide discounts for pensioners, students, or holders of Interail or Eurail cards. For visitors arriving from Russia there are two express trains daily from St Petersburg and one from Moscow to Helsinki.

Helsinki Railway Station

By boat

The best routes to Finland by boat are from Sweden and Germany. Silja Line and Viking Line operate daily services between Stockholm and Helsinki. These ferries are state-of-the-art vessels equipped with restaurants, saunas, swimming pools, tax-free shops, and children's playrooms. Superfast ferries (www.superfast.com) make the trip between Rostok in Germany and Hanko in Finland in 22 hours.

A local ferry

It's slightly cheaper to travel by ferry from Stockholm to Turku or Naantali in western Finland and then overland to Helsinki rather than by direct ship to Helsinki. Other lines, such as RG Line, run services between Vaasa in Finland and Umeå in Sweden to points further north than the Stockholm and Turku areas. For information on sea travel contact any Helsinki travel agent.

By car

If you want to take your own car, probably the easiest route from Northern Europe is via Germany and Estonia (ferry: Rostock–Tallinn–Helsinki) or from Britain by ferry from Harwich to Sweden. In Sweden the E4 main road follows the Gulf of Bothnia through Sweden and on into Finland. This is a good route if you want to visit northern Sweden, northern Finland and/or Lapland. The border crossing between the twin towns of Haparanda in Sweden and Tornio in Finland is about 1,020 km (634 miles) north of Stockholm at the head of the Gulf of Bothnia.

It is also possible to drive to Finland via the three Baltic States – no visas are required for Lithuania, Latvia and Estonia. The route takes you through Poland, Kaunas (Lithuania) and St Petersburg to the Russian–Finnish border at Vaalimaa or Nuijamaa.

The distance from Berlin to Helsinki via Warsaw and St Petersburg is just under 2,500 km (1,554 miles). Another route is to go via Poland and Kaunas (avoid Kaliningrad at all costs!) and Riga (Latvia's capital) to Tallinn. From Tallinn there are several passenger ferries a day to Helsinki.

Travelling by bus to Finland from the Continent is a trek but it can be done. Enquire at the Finnish Tourist Board in your home country.

Getting to the Åland Islands

There are regular flight connections to the Åland Islands from Helsinki and Turku. From Sweden there are car ferry connections from Stockholm and Kapellskär to Mariehamn, and from Grisslehamn to Eckerö, the westernmost group of islands. Those who feel like doing a spot of island-hopping before even arriving should take a ferry from Osnäs or Korpo, two islands off Turku.

*Some ferries take cars
Traversing Åland*

Getting Around

By car

The main roads in Finland all have asphalt surfaces; the side roads generally don't. Sand- or gravel-covered roads are regularly maintained and are generally comfortable to drive along, though beware of sharp bends and steep gradients. All major roads are marked with white numbers (European routes are green, main trunk roads are red and all other roads are blue).

No special documents are needed apart from a national driving licence, vehicle papers and a country sticker on the back of the car. A green international insurance card is recommended but not compulsory. The speed limit in built-up areas is 50kph (30mph) and sometimes lower, on country roads 80kph (50mph), and on motorways 100kph (60mph) during winter and 120kph (70mph) in summer. Caravans are not allowed to go faster than 80kph (50mph). Outside built-up areas all vehicles need to drive with their sidelights and/or headlights on at all times. Seat-belts are compulsory for everyone. Drink-driving laws are very strict.

Traffic signs are similar to those in the rest of Europe. Vehicles coming from the right have priority unless otherwise indicated, and in the smaller villages a yellow triangle with a red edge means 'give way'. In Helsinki, trams always have priority over all other traffic.

Be very careful when signs portraying wild animals appear. Elk and reindeer are fond of crossing roads, especially at twilight. Should a collision occur, notify the police immediately (tel: 112); ambulances can also be summoned using this number. Accidents should be reported to the Finnish Motor Insurers' Centre, Buleardi 28, 00120 Helsinki; tel: 09-680401, which is responsible for taking care of accidents involving foreign vehicles.

All the major car rental companies are represented at the main airports and cities. A valid driving licence and a minimum age of between 19 and 24 (depending on company) are compulsory. Medium-priced rental cars cost €35–50 per day (including a rate per km of roughly €0.5–€0.7); campers and mobile homes cost around €900 per week (price includes 2,000km).

Bicycle hire

Bicycle hire *(Polkupyöränvuokraus)* is available at hotels, youth hostels, campsites, holiday villages, sports shops, travel agencies and also several local tourist offices.

Taxis

Taxis have a yellow sign on the top saying Taksi. For numbers of the taxi ranks, look under "taksi" in the phone book.

Planning itineraries

Hammarland bridge

A good alternative in towns

By air

Finnair has a comprehensive network of domestic connections. The 'Finnair Holiday Ticket', which is valid for 30 days, provides unlimited use of domestic flights. For further information contact a Finnair office or your travel agent.

By train

Finland's rail network (www.vr.fi) covers a total distance of roughly 6,000km (3,700 miles), but is only really comprehensive in the southern part of the country. Lapland can be reached by train: the Helsinki–Rovaniemi route can be covered in around 10 hours, and also features a very handy motorail service which operates all year round. Rail prices in Finland tend to be less expensive than in some other European countries.

A Finnrail Pass is valid on all trains, and comes in 3-, 5- or 10-day versions. These passes aren't transferable though. Euro Domino railpasses allow between 3 and 10 days unlimited rail travel in Finland, but they need to be purchased before arrival.

Other international rail tickets and cards accepted by the Finnish rail network include Eurail Pass, Eurail Young Pass, Eurail Flexipass, Scanrail Pass, InterRail cards and the Rail Europe Senior card.

By bus

The Finnish bus network covers the whole country; the north-south bus routes (for example Helsinki–Jyväskylä–Oulu–Rovaniemi) are often preferable to the railways because of their flexible routes, which can also include the smallest of villages. Prices are lower than those of the railways. There are always a number of special discount tickets available.

By boat

Take a nostalgic trip

Getting around by ferry can be fun even although it tends to be somewhat slow. Many of the ferries are well fitted out and are rather like excursion ships or cruise ships, and are usually available only during the peak season (mid-June to mid-August). Old steamships and paddle-steamers provide a nostalgic alternative.

In Helsinki

The **Helsinki Card** allows unlimited travel on public transport in the capital for 24, 48 or 72 hours, free admission to over 50 museums and sights, and discounts on certain accommodation.

These cards can be purchased from the city tourist information office, Pohjoisesplanadi 19, tel: 09-169 3757, fax: 169 3839, e-mail: tourist.info@hel.fi

Facts for the Visitor

Travel documents

Bring a passport or identity card. Visas are not required for nationals of European Union member countries or the USA.

Customs regulations

Goods from countries in the EU destined for personal use can be taken freely in and out of Finland by EU citizens, although there is a limit on alcohol and tobacco. The following allowances apply to goods or travellers from non-EU countries: 200 cigarettes or 250g tobacco; 1 litre alcoholic beverages above 22 percent or 2 litres alcohol below 22 percent; 60ml perfume or 250ml eau de toilette. Antiques more than 50 years old may only be taken out of the country with the prior permission of the Finnish Museums Central Administration, Nervanderinkatu 13, 00100 Helsinki.

Finnish symbol

Currency regulations

Foreign currency may be taken in or out of the country in unlimited amounts.

Tourist information

Information can be obtained from the offices of the Finnish Tourist Board at the following addresses:

In the UK: 30–35 Pall Mall, London, SW1Y 5LP; tel: 020-7365 2512; fax: 020-8600 5681. E-mail: finlandinfo.lon@mek.fi

Finland welcomes tourists

In the US: 655 Third Avenue, New York, NY 10017; tel: 212-885 9737; fax: 212-885 9710; mek.usa@mek.fi

In Finland: Eteläesplanadi 4, 00130 Helsinki; tel: 09-4176 9300; fax: 09-4176 9301. Also at Pohjoisesplanadi 19, FIN-00100 Helsinki; tel: 09-169 3757; fax: 09-169 3839; www.hel.fi In Turku: Aurakatu 4, 20100 Turku; tel: 02-262 7444; fax: 02-262 7674. For general information check out the website: www.finland-tourism.com or www.travel.fi

Detailed information on the various festivals across the country may be obtained from Finland Festivals, Uudenmaankatu 36D21, 00120 Helsinki, tel: 09-612 6760, fax: 09-612 7610, www.festivals.fi

Tour guides

Tour guides, who are known as *opas*, can be provided by the local and regional tourist offices. These offices also provide information on regular guided tour services and local events.

Currency and exchange

The Finnish unit of currency is the *euro*. Notes and coins are as in other euro countries except that 1 and 2 cent coins are not minted nor used. They are accepted, though, but must be given at 5-cent amounts at a time. All banks and many hotels have currency exchange facilities; rates in hotels tend to be less favourable. Many hotels, restaurants and shops accept credit cards and traveller's cheques.

Tipping
Taxi drivers do not expect tips, nor do waiters and barkeepers, because service is included in the price. If you're very satisfied with your waiter or waitress, however, they certainly don't mind being given a bit extra. Porters at stations expect to be tipped, along with porters in hotels and restaurants (€1).

Opening times
Shops in Finland are generally open Monday to Friday 9am–6pm; larger stores and supermarkets *(automarket/ ostoskeskus)* stay open until 8pm, and are open on Saturday from 9am–2pm. Many shops in city centres are closed during the summer, but grocery stores remain open in the suburbs and in rural areas *(lähikauppa/kyläkauppa)*, also on Saturday and Sunday. All the filling stations in Finland now do lead-free petrol, and tend to be open from 7am–8pm. Some close earlier on Sunday, but often have automatic machines that operate with banknotes.

Banks are open Monday to Friday 9.15am–4.15pm; the airport branches are open 6.30am–11pm; in Katajanokka Harbour, 9–11.30am and 3.45–6pm; in Turku Harbour 8–11.30am and 7.30–9.30pm; and the exchange outlets at the central station in Helsinki are open daily from 8am–9pm. Post offices are open Monday to Friday 9am–5pm.

Clothing
In summertime, be sure to bring a pullover and rainwear too. Hikers need sturdy shoes, and those headed for Lapland should bring Wellington boots. In winter bring several warm pullovers, an anorak, skiing clothes, thick socks, gloves, a hat and 'snowproof' boots. The Finns are very relaxed about clothes, and hardly any restaurants have strict dress codes.

A variety of souvenirs

Souvenirs
Good souvenirs from Finland include glassware, jewellery, pottery and other craft articles, fashion goods and furs.

Public holidays
The official public holidays are: 1 January (New Year's day); 6 January (Epiphany); Good Friday and Easter Sunday; 30 April–1 May (Vappu Festival); 25 May (Ascension); Whitsun; 1 November (All Saints' Day); 6 December (Independence Day); 24–26 December (Christmas).

Postal services

Stamps can be bought at post offices *(posti/post)*, at stamp machines, stationery shops and hotels. Ordinary letters and postcards to the UK and the rest of the EU from Finland cost €0.60 each.

Telephone

Coin-operated public phones are a rarity in Finland these days; post offices and kiosks all sell phonecards.

To make an international call from Finland, dial 00, 999 or 994 first, then the country code: UK 44; US and Canada 1. To ring Finland from abroad, dial 00358, then the area code (minus the 0) and the number.

AT&T: 9800-100-10;
MCI: 9800-102-80;
Sprint: 9800-102-84.

Finnish postbox

Media

Foreign newspapers are available from the main railway station bookstores and 'R' kiosks in all the major cities. The news in English is broadcast once a day in Helsinki on 103.7 FM.

95

Time

Finland is on East European time, ie. two hours ahead of Greenwich Mean Time, seven hours ahead of Eastern Standard Time in the US. It also follows the European daylight saving time in summer.

Voltage, weights and measures

The voltage in Finland is 220v. Bring along an adaptor. Finland uses the decimal system, therefore all distances are measured in kilometres.

The disabled

One third of all hotel rooms in Finland have been equipped with the disabled in mind. There are also special cabins on Baltic ferries, and disabled toilets at most service areas and in many restaurants. Ramps are also provided at several sights and in public buildings. For more information, contact Rullaten, Pajutie 7, 02770 Espoo; tel: 09-805 7393; fax: 09-855 2470.

Medical

No special vaccinations are necessary for trips to Finland. Treatment in the outpatients departments of local health centres, known as *terveyskeskus*, and polyclinics, is free – apart from small local fees.

Visitors from EU countries are entitled to medical treatment in Finland under a reciprocal agreement, but they should make sure they have form E111 issued in their own country. All other travellers should take out medical insurance for their trip. Further information can be provided by health insurance companies.

Medicine can be bought at chemists (*apteekki*, Monday to Friday 9am–6pm, Saturday 9am–2pm, emergency chemists until 10pm).

Mosquitoes
Finland is unfortunately rather popular with mosquitoes – only at the height of summer, though, and mostly in Northern Finland and Lapland, where they tend to be a persistent nuisance. Your best chance of avoiding them is to keep clothing buttoned up. Local chemists and supermarkets stock tried and tested repellents and know their own brand of insect.

Emergencies
The main emergency number is 112, and the police can be reached on 10022. For emergency medical attention in Helsinki, tel: 1008, and for emergency dental treatment tel: 736166.

Local emergency numbers in other cities and towns can be obtained from tourist offices and hotels.

Lost and found
In rural areas, lost articles may be recovered either from police stations (*nimismies*) or lost property offices (*löytötavaratoimisto*). In Helsinki contact: Päijänteentie 12A, 3rd floor, tel: 09-189 3180.

Diplomatic representation
British Embassy, 170 Itainen Puistotie, 00140, Helsinki; tel: 09-22865100. US Embassy 14b Itainen Puistotie, 00140, Helsinki; tel: 09-171931.

Welcome to Lapland

Accommodation

Hotels in Finland are generally of a very high standard; the rooms usually have separate bathrooms, radios, televisions and telephones. There's always a sauna, often with a swimming pool. Hotel restaurants serve hot food late, and the room price includes the breakfast buffet. Reliable hotel chains with establishments in almost every major town are Scandic, Sokos and Cumulus-Rantasipi.

Hotel vouchers (available from travel agencies and tour operators) can cut down prices quite a bit. The 'Finncheque' system (valid from 1 June until 30 September) is honoured by over 140 hotels and allows holders to spend one night in a double room (breakfast included) in a category III hotel for a basic fixed rate. This is ideal for young families as children under the age of 4 can sleep in their parents' room for no extra charge. Booking for the next hotel is also free.

Here is a list of recommended hotels along the routes described in this book. They fall roughly into the following price categories: €€€ = expensive, €€ = moderate and € = cheap.

Rural accommodation

97

Eckerö
€€€Hotel Havsbandet, Eckerö, tel: 018-38200, fax: 38305; **€€Eckerö Hotell**, Eckerö, tel: 018-38447, fax: 38247.

Ekenäs (Tammisaari)
€€€Strandhotell, Pohjankatu 2, tel: 019-246 1500, fax: 246 1505.

Espoo
€€€Hanasaari, tel: 09-435020, fax: 467291, hanasaari@hanaholmen/fi out on a peninsula; **€€€Siikaranta**, Siikajärvi, tel: 09-867971, fax; 867 97455, beautifully situated; **€Finnhotel Espoo**, Napurinkalliontie 3, tel: 09-8678810, fax: 8670355.

Espoo town centre

Hämeenlinna
€€€Vaakuna, Possentie 7, tel: 03-65831, fax: 658 3600, right on Lake Vanajavesi, good restaurant.

Hamina
€€€Haminan Seurahuone, Pikkuympyräkatu 5, tel: 05-35035, centrally situated with good restaurant; **€€Summer Hotel Anna**, Annankatu 1, tel: 05-354 1600; only in summer (1 June to 15 August).

Hanko
€€€Regatta, Merikatu 1, tel: 019-248 6491, fax: 248 5535, 50 yards from the beach.

Hotel Grand Marina

Heinola
€€€**Hotel Kumpeli**, Muonamiehenkatu 3, tel: 03-715 8214, fax: 715 8899; Kumpeli@sci.fi; €€**Finnhostel Heinola**, Opintie 1, tel: 03-714 1655; finnhostelheinola@iobox.fi summer only.

Helsinki
€€€**Grand Marina**, Katajanokanlaituri 7, tel: 09-16661, fax: 664764, CSCE conference centre; €€€**Lordhotel**, Lönnrotinkatu 29, tel: 09-615815, fax: 680 1315, in art nouveau castle, excellent cellar restaurant; €€**Omapohja**, Itäinen Teatterikuja 3, tel: 09-666211, fax: 622 80053, near the station; €€**Apartement Ruut**, Töölönkatu 26, tel: 050-594 113, fax: 447757, good alternative to a hotel; €**Stadion Hostel**, Pohjoinen Stadionintie 3, tel: 09-477 8480, fax: 09-447 84811, stadion@hostel.inet.fi, in the 1950-Olympics Stadium building.

Hetta
€€€**Jussan Tupa**, Hetta, tel: 016-521101, fax: 521379, cosy.

Iisalmi
€€€**Hotel Artos**, Kyllikinkatu 8, tel: 017-812244, fax: 814941, same building as the Evakkokeskus; €€€**Seurahuone**, Savonkatu 24, tel: 017-83831, fax: 823565, near the Evakkokeskus; €**Hostel**, Sarvikatu 4c, tel: 017-823940.

Ilomantsi
€€€**Pääskynpesä**, Henrikintie 4, tel: 013-6821200, fax: 682 1444, centrally located with good restaurant.

Imatra
€€€**Scandic Hotel Valtionhotelli**, Torkkelinkatu 2, tel: 05-68881, fax: 688 8888, imatra@scandic-hotels.com luxury lodge built by Tsar Nicholas I in 1845; €€**Rantahovi**, golf course, tel: 05-473 4944, next to Lake Immolanjärvi.

Joensuu
€€€**Atrium**, Siltakatu 4, tel: 013-126911, fax: 226969, with Viennese-style restaurant; €€€**Sokos Hotel Vaakuna**, Torikatu 20, tel: 013-277511, fax: 277 3210, on market square with pub and disco; €**Finnhostel Joensuu**, Kalevankatu 8, tel: 013-267 5076, fax: 267 5075, finnhostel @islo.jns.fi

Jyväskylä
€€**Scandic Hotel Jyväskylä**, Vapaudenkatu 73, tel: 014-330 3000, fax: 616996, Jyväskylä@scandic-hotels.com, best hotel in town; €€€**Sokos Hotel Jyväshovi**, Kauppakatu 35,

tel: 014-413 3200, fax: 413 3290, in the pedestrian area;
€€Hotel Milton, Hannikaisenkatu 29, tel: 014-213411, fax:
631927, by station.

Karstula
€€Hotel Harkko, Keskustie 7, tel: 014-61311, cosy.

Kemi
€€€Merihovi, Keskuspuistokatu 6-8, tel: 016-223431,
fax: 228299, well-appointed and central; **€€Motel Yöpuu**,
Eteläntie 227, tel/fax: 016-232034.

Keuruu
€€Keurusselkä, tel: 014-75100, fax: 738008, lakeside,
good restaurant.

Kilpisjärvi
€€Hotel Kilpis, tel/fax: 016-537761, info@kilpis-hotel.com.

Kokkola
€€€Grand Hotel, Pitkänsillankatu 28, tel/fax: 06-831
3411, on the Sunti river; **€€€Sokos Hotel Kaarle**, Kauppatori 4, tel: 06-826 6111, fax: 826 6490, hotelli.kauppatori
@co.inet.fi in market square.

Kotka
€€€Sokos Hotel Seurahuone, Keskuskatu 21, tel: 05-
350 35, fax: 350 0450, centrally located; **€€€Leikari**,
Rantahaka, in Karhula, tel: 05-227 8111, fax: 285803,
hotelli.leikari@co.inet.fi at junction of roads 7 and 15.

Kristiinankaupunki
€€€Kristina, Stortorget 1, tel: 06-221 2555, fax: 221
3250, near the sea.

Kuopio
€€€Cumulus, Puijonkatu 32, tel: 017-617711, fax: 617
7299, kuopio.cumulus@restel.fi near the railway station;
€€€Kuopion Keskushotelli, Haapaniemenkatu 20, tel:
017-261 8800, fax: 261 8811, on market square; **€€Rauhalahti**, Katiskaniementie 8, tel: 017-473473, fax: 473470,
myynti@rauholahti.com Rauhalahti: spa hotel, with a camping ground and a youth hostel nearby.

Kuusamo
€€€Sokos Hotel Kuusamo, tel: 08-85920, fax: 852 1263,
Lapland flair with Sami food in the restaurant; **€€Kuusamon Tropiikki**, Kylpyläntie, tel: 08-85960, fax: 852 1909,
comfortable apartments; **€€Kuusamon Asuntohotelli**,
Juhantie 10, tel: 08-852 3619, fax: 852 2977, centrally
located.

Marina in Kotka

Kristiinankaupunki

Lahti
€€€Cumulus Lahti, Vapaudenkatu 24, tel: 03-813711, fax: 781 8922, near the theatre; **€€€Lahden Seurahuone**, Aleksanterinkatu 14, tel: 03-85111, fax: 752 3164, centrally located.

Lappeenranta
€€€Cumulus, Valtakatu 31, tel: 05-677811, fax: 677 8299, lappeenranta.cumulus@restel.fi on the market square.

Lieksa
€€Aigabriha, Honkatie 3, tel: 013-522922, guest-house style; **€€Loma-Kitsi**, Kitsintie 86a, tel/fax: 013-539114, top-class holiday apartments. **€Kestikievari Herranniemi**, Lieksa Vuonislahti, tel: 013-542110, fax: 542153, idyllically situated on Lake Pielinen.

Loviisa
€€Degerby, Brandensteininkatu 17, tel: 019-531725, fax: 505 6200.

Mariehamn
€€€Åland Hotel Adlon, Hamngatan 7, tel: 018-15300, fax: 15077, next to ferry; **€€€Arkipelag**, Strandgatan 31, tel: 018-24020, fax: 27384, nightlife hotspot; **€€€Park Alandia Hotel**, N Esplanadgatan 3, tel: 018-14130, fax: 17130; **€€Esplanad**, Storagatan 5, tel: 018-16444, fax: 14143; **€€Strandnäs**, Godbyvägen, tel: 018-21511, fax: 21955.

Mikkeli
€€€Sokos Hotel Vaakuna, Porrassalmenkatu 9, tel: 015-20201, fax: 202 0421, no-smoking floor; **€€€Cumulus**, Mikonkatu 9, tel: 015-20511, fax: 205 1299, mikkeli.cumulus@restel.fi, centrally located; **€€Varsavuori**, Kirkonvarkaus, tel: 015-410 4100 hvarsaru@nettilinja.fi on Lake Saimaa.

Naantali
€€€Naantali Spa Hotel, Matkailijantie 2, tel: 02-44550, fax: 445 5622; info@naantalispa.fi **€€Wahvan Paronin Majatalo**, Mannerheiminkatu 7, tel: 02-435 3722, fax: 435 2712, romantic rooms.

Nurmes
€€€Bomba Holidays Spa, Suojärvenkatu 1, tel: 013-687200, fax: 687 2100, Karelian food buffet for €14. **€€** Hyvärilä, Flomatiel, tel: 013-481770, fax: 013-481 775, rooms and camping.

Orivesi
€€Hotel Orivesi, Keskustie 40, tel: 03-377 6400, fax: 03-334 0667, hotelliorivesi@hotelliorivesi.fi central location.

Oulu
€€€Best Western Apollo, Asemakatu 31-33, tel: 08-379555, fax: 372060; **€€€ Oulun Eden**, by the sea in Nallikari, tel: 08-550 4100, fax: 554 4103, conference hotel and spa; **€€Turisti**, Rautatienkatu 9, tel: 08-375233, fax: 311 0755, good value town hotel;

Pietarsaari
€€€Hotel Vega, Alholmintie 9, tel: 06-723 5028, 2km/1 mile from the centre, near the boat harbour; **€Hostel Svanen/Joutsen**, Nissarön, tel: 06-723 0660, svanen@multi.fi 4km/2 miles from the centre, also has campsite.

Pori
€€€Yyteri Spa Hotel, Yyteri, 02-628 5300, fax: 638 3776, popular hotel; **€Tekunkorpi**, Tekniikantie 4b, tel: 02-637 8400, hostel.

Porvoo
€€Sparre, Piispankatu 34, tel: 019-584455, fax: 584465, near the old town, good restaurant.

Rauma
€€€Kalliohovi, kalliohovi@kalliohovi.fi Kalliokatu 25, tel: 02-83881, fax: 83882400, comfortable hotel, all the mod cons, centrally located; **€€€Best Western Hotel Raumanlinna**, Valtakatu 5, tel: 02-83221, fax: 02-83222111, raumanlinna@raumanlinna.fi, also has a good restaurant; **€€Cityhovi**, Nortamonkatu 18, tel: 02-822 3745, fax: 822 3742, typical town hotel.

101

Rustic Rauma

Rovaniemi
€€€Hotel Pohjanhovi, Pohjanpuistikko 2, tel: 016-33711, fax: 313997, pohjanhovirantasipi@restel.fi traditional hotel, large dance-restaurant; **€€€Sokos Hotel Vaakuna**, Koskikatu 4, tel: 016-332211, fax: 332 2199, bastion of Rovaniemi nightlife; **€€Matka Borealis**, Asemieskatu 1, tel/fax: 016-342 0130, near the railway station; **€€Ounasvaaran Pirtit Holiday Village**, Ounasvaara Ski Centre, tel: 016-369056, fax: 369061, well appointed cabins on mountain slope.

Speedy Saarijärvi

Savonlinna
€€€Casino Spa Hotel, Kasinosaari, tel: 015-7395430, fax: 272524, beautifully situated in this lake landscape; **€€Vuorilinna**, Kasinosaari, tel: 015-739 5495, very pleasant, open summer only.

Seinäjoki
€€€Sokos Hotel Lakeus, Torikatu 2, tel: 06-419 5111, fax: 419 5190, centrally located with steak bar;

€€€Cumulus, Kauppakatu 10, tel: 06-418 6111, fax: 418 6299, also has good restaurant; **€€€Hotel Sorsanpesä**, Törnäväntie 27, tel: 06-419 9111, fax: 419 9299, by the river; **€Vuorela Guest House**, Kalevankatu 31, tel: 06-423 2195.

Tampere
€€€Sokos Hotel Ilves, Hataanpäänvaltatie 1, 03-2626262, fax: 262 6263, next to the Tammerkoski Rapids; **€€€Tampereen Kylpylä Hotel**, Lapinniemenranta 12, tel: 03-259 7500, fax: 259 7400, luxury spa hotel; **€€Summer Hotel Härmälä**, Leirintäkatu 8, tel: 03-265 1355, next to Pyhäjärvi Lake, 4km (2½ miles) out of town; **€€€Sokos Hotel Villa**, Sumeliuksenkatu 14, tel: 03-262 6267, fax: 262 6268, town centre; **€Hostel Uimahallin Maja**, Pirkankatu 10–12, tel: 03-2229460, fax: 222 9940, sales@hosteltampere.com summer hotel and youth hostel.

Turku
€€€Seaport Hotel, Ferry Harbour, tel: 02-283 3000, fax: 283 3100; **€€€Scandic Hotel Marina Palace**, Linnankatu 32, tel: 02-336300, fax: 251 6750, centrally situated, good seafood restaurant; **€Hostel**, Linnankatu 39, tel: 02-262 7680, fax: 262 7675, by the river.

Uusikaupunki
€€€Aquarius, Kullervontie 11b, tel: 02-841 3123, fax: 841 3540, hotelli.aquarius@uusikaupunki.fi close to market square; **€€Lännentie**, Levysepänkatu 1, tel: 02-841 2636, fax: 841 2651, also has cheaper hostel section (**€**).

Vaasa
€€€Radisson SAS Royal Hotel Vaasa, Hovioikeuden-puistikko 18, tel: 212811, fax 06-312 3861, near the station; **€€€Tropiclandia**, Lemmenpolku 3, tel: 06-283 8000, fax: 06-283 8888; **€Tekla**, Palosaarentie 58, tel: 06-327 6411, fax: 321 3989, hostel.

Varkaus
€€€Oscar, Kauppatori 4, tel: 017-579011, fax: 579 0500, hotel.oscar@varkaudenhotellit.fi, first-class, centrally situated.

Camping close to nature

Viitasaari
€€€Hotel Pihkuri, Kappelitie 5, tel: 014-577 7500, fax: 577 7555, on Lake Keitele.

Camping
Finland's campsites are close to nature – usually right next to lakes – and are ideal for family holidays because of the vast range of activities available. All the sites are inspected regularly and are classified on a star system of one to three. Peak season runs from Midsummer Night

until the end of July, and prices are between €5–20 a day. Gas canisters can be refilled or exchanged at a few sites, but the best place to go is the nearest filling station; butane cannot be purchased in Finland. Many campsites have a selection of wooden camping huts on their premises, usually quite simple affairs with a small cooker and a fridge, though some have saunas, showers and lavatories too.

Youth hostel

Youth hostels

The Finnish word for a youth hostel is *hostel*, and they come in three categories. The price per night is usually between €10 and €25, depending on the location and facilities available, www.srmnet.org

Summer hotels

Finland's cheap summer hotels are a special feature of the country: they are student hostels which open their doors to tourists during the summer holiday from 1 June to 31 August. It's certainly not luxury accommodation, but all the necessaries are provided.

Farmhouse holidays

As well as providing accommodation, most farms are situated next to lakes or rivers and are ideal for fishing, rowing, hiking and hunting holidays. The guest rooms are either in the main building or in separate cabins, and there's usually a choice between self-catering or eating with the farmer's family. The use of the sauna is always included.

103

Guest houses

These are usually family-run, and are a cheap alternative to hotels. They come in all shapes and sizes, from small family homes with just a few rooms to large hotel-like affairs, often with restaurants attached.

Holiday home

Motels

Finland's motels are usually on main roads, but always in delightful surroundings. They provide average accommodation at reasonable prices. Some motels have holiday cabins on their premises, simply equipped for overnight stays.

Holiday homes

Renting a holiday home, or *mökki*, is great in the summer. Chopping wood, heating up the sauna and frying fish straight from the river all add to the experience. Most of Finland's 200 holiday villages and 10,000 private holiday houses are in the central and northern part of the Lake Region. There's one to suit all tastes, from the modest little hut to the luxury bungalow with whirlpool and cable TV. All buildings have water and a place to cook, and basic equipment includes kitchenware, a sauna (usually) and a boat.

Index